TO

FRANCIS LANDEY PATTON

THIS BOOK IS DEDICATED

AS AN INADEQUATE BUT HEARTFELT EXPRESSION

OF

GRATITUDE AND RESPECT

WHAT IS FAITH?

BY

J. GRESHAM MACHEN, D.D., Litt.D.

PROFESSOR OF NEW TESTAMENT IN WESTMINSTER THEOLOGICAL
SEMINARY, PHILADELPHIA

WM. B. EERDMANS PUBLISHING COMPANY
GRAND RAPIDS, MICHIGAN

First paperback edition, September 1962
Second printing, August 1965
Third printing, July 1969
Fourth printing, November 1972
Fifth printing, March 1974

ISBN 0-8028-1122-1

PREFACE

This book contains the material of a course of lectures which was delivered at the Grove City Bible School in the summer of 1925. More or less extensive use has been made of articles contributed by the author to *The Princeton Theological Review, The New York Times, The Real Issue* (published by the Philadelphian Society of Princeton University), and *Christian Education* (an article published also in *The Sunday School Times*). A paper entitled "Faith and Knowledge," which was published in the *Bulletin* of the Fourth Biennial Meeting (held in June, 1924) of the Conference of Theological Seminaries and Colleges in the United States and Canada, has been incorporated in greater part in the course of Chapters I, III, and VIII. By kind permission of the Editor of *The Woman's Home Companion*, use has been made, in Chapter II, of several paragraphs of an article on "My Idea of God" that appeared in that journal for December, 1925.

CONTENTS

WHAT IS FAITH?

CHAPTER I

INTRODUCTION

The question, "What is Faith?", which forms the subject of the following discussion may seem to some persons impertinent and unnecessary. Faith, it may be said, cannot be known except by experience, and when it is known by experience logical analysis of it, and logical separation of it from other experiences, will only serve to destroy its power and its charm. The man who knows by experience what it is to trust Christ, for example, to rest upon Him for salvation, will never need, it may be held, to engage in psychological investigations of that experience which is the basis of his life; and indeed such investigations may even serve to destroy the thing that is to be investigated.

Such objections are only one manifestation of a tendency that is very widespread at the present day, the tendency to disparage the intellectual aspect of the religious life. Religion, it is held, is an ineffable experience; the intellectual expression of it can be symbolical merely; the most various opinions in the religious sphere are compatible with a fundamental unity of life; theology may vary and yet religion may remain the same.

Obviously this temper of mind is hostile to precise definitions. Indeed nothing makes a man more unpopular in the controversies of the present day than an insistence upon definition of terms. Anything, it seems, may be forgiven more readily than that. Men discourse very eloquently today upon such subjects as God, religion, Christianity, atonement, redemption, faith; but are greatly incensed when they are asked to tell in simple language what they mean by these terms. They do not like to have the flow of their eloquence checked by so vulgar a thing as a definition. And so they will probably be incensed by the question which forms the title of the present book; in the midst of eloquent celebrations of faith—usually faith contrasted with knowledge—it seems disconcerting to be asked what faith is.

This anti-intellectual tendency in the modern world is no trifling thing; it has its roots deep in the entire philosophical development of modern times. Modern philosophy since the days of Kant, with the theology that has been influenced by it, has had as its dominant note, certainly as its present-day result, a depreciation of the reason and a skeptical answer to Pilate's question, "What is truth?" This attack upon the intellect has been conducted by men of marked intellectual power; but an attack upon the intellect it has been all the same. And at last the logical results of it, even in the sphere of practice, are beginning to appear. A marked characteristic of the present day is a lamentable intellectual decline, which has appeared in all fields of human endeavor except those that deal with purely material things. The intellect has been browbeaten so long in theory that one cannot be surprised if it is now ceasing to function in practice. Schleiermacher and

Ritschl, despite their own intellectual gifts, have, it may fairly be maintained, contributed largely to produce that indolent impressionism which, for example in the field of New Testament studies, has largely taken the place of the patient researches of a generation or so ago.

The intellectual decadence of the day is not limited to the Church, or to the subject of religion, but appears in secular education as well. Sometimes it is assisted by absurd pedagogic theories, which, whatever their variety in detail, are alike in their depreciation of the labor of learning facts. Facts, in the sphere of education, are having a hard time. The old-fashioned notion of reading a book or hearing a lecture and simply storing up in the mind what the book or the lecture contains— this is regarded as entirely out of date. A year or so ago I heard a noted educator give some advice to a company of college professors—advice which was typical of the present tendency in education. It is a great mistake, he said in effect, to suppose that a college professor ought to teach; on the contrary he ought simply to give the students an opportunity to learn.

This pedagogic theory of following the line of least resistance in education and avoiding all drudgery and all hard work has been having its natural result; it has joined forces with the natural indolence of youth to produce in present-day education a very lamentable decline.

The decline has not, indeed, been universal; in the sphere of the physical sciences, for example, the acquisition of facts is not regarded as altogether out of date. Indeed, the anti-intellectualistic tendency in religion and in those subjects that deal specifically with the things of the spirit has been due, partly at least, to a monopolistic possession of the intellect on the part of the physical sciences and of their utilitarian applications. But in the long run it is to be questioned whether even those branches of endeavor will profit by their monopolistic claims; in the long run the intellect will hardly profit by being excluded from the higher interests of the human spirit, and its decadence may then appear even in the material sphere.

But however that may be, whether or not intellectual decadence has already extended or will soon extend to the physical sciences, its prevalence in other spheres—in literature and history, for example, and still more clearly in the study of language—is perfectly plain. An outstanding feature of contemporary education in these spheres is the growth of ignorance; pedagogic theory and the growth of ignorance have gone hand in hand.

The undergraduate student of the present day is being told that he need not take notes on what he hears in class, that the exercise of the memory is a rather childish and mechanical thing, and that what he is really in college to do is to think for himself and to unify his world. He usually makes a poor business of unifying his world. And the reason is clear. He does not succeed in unifying his world for the simple reason that he has no world to unify. He has not acquired a knowledge of a sufficient number of facts in order even to learn the method of putting facts together. He is being told to practise the business of mental digestion;

but the trouble is that he has no food to digest. The modern student, contrary to what is often said, is really being starved for want of facts.

Certainly we are not discouraging originality. On the contrary we desire to encourage it in every possible way, and we believe that the encouragement of it will be of immense benefit to the spread of the Christian religion. The trouble with the university students of the present day, from the point of view of evangelical Christianity, is not that they are too original, but that they are not half original enough. They go on in the same routine way, following their leaders like a flock of sheep, repeating the same stock phrases with little knowledge of what they mean, swallowing whole whatever professors choose to give them—and all the time imagining that they are bold, bad, independent young men, merely because they abuse what everybody else is abusing, namely, the religion that is founded upon Christ. It is popular today to abuse that unpopular thing that is known as supernatural Christianity, but original it certainly is not. A true originality might bring some resistance to the current of the age, some willingness to be unpopular, and some independent scrutiny, at least, if not acceptance, of the claims of Christ. If there is one thing more than another which we believers in historic Christianity ought to encourage in the youth of our day it is independence of mind.

It is a great mistake, then, to suppose that we who are called "conservatives" hold desperately to certain beliefs merely because they are old, and are opposed to the discovery of new facts. On the contrary, we welcome new discoveries with all our hearts, and we believe that our cause will come to its rights again only when youth throws off its present intellectual lethargy, refuses to go thoughtlessly with the anti-intellectual current of the age, and recovers some genuine independence of mind. In one sense, indeed, we are traditionalists; we do maintain that any institution that is really great has its roots in the past; we do not therefore desire to substitute modern sects for the historic Christian Church. But on the whole, in view of the conditions that now exist, it would perhaps be more correct to call us "radicals" than to call us "conservatives." We look not for a mere continuation of spiritual conditions that now exist, but for an outburst of new power; we are seeking in particular to arouse youth from its present uncritical repetition of current phrases into some genuine examination of the basis of life; and we believe that Christianity flourishes not in the darkness, but in the light. A revival of the Christian religion, we believe, will deliver mankind from its present bondage, and like the great revival of the sixteenth century will bring liberty to mankind. Such a revival will be not the work of man, but the work of the Spirit of God. But one of the means which the Spirit will use, we believe, is an awakening of the intellect. The retrograde, anti-intellectual movement called Modernism, a movement which really degrades the intellect by excluding it from the sphere of religion, will be overcome, and thinking will again come to its rights. The new Reformation, in other words, will be accompained by a new Renaissance; and the last thing in the world that we desire to do is to discourage originality or independence of mind.

But what we do insist upon is that the right to originality has to be earned, and that it cannot be earned by ignorance or by indolence. A man cannot be original in his treatment of a subject unless he knows what the subject is; true originality is preceded by patient attention to the facts. It is that patient attention to the facts which, in application of modern pedagogic theory, is being neglected by the youth of the present day.

In our insistence upon mastery of facts in education, we are sometimes charged with the desire of forcing our opinions ready-made upon our students. We professors get up behind our professorial desks, it is said, and proceed to lecture. The helpless students are expected not only to listen but to take notes; then they are expected to memorize what we have said, with all our firstly's and secondly's and thirdly's; and finally they are expected to give it all back to us in the examination. Such a system—so the charge runs—stifles all originality and all life. Instead, the modern pedagogical expert comes with a message of hope; instead of memorizing facts, he says, true education consists in learning to think; drudgery is a thing of the past, and self-expression is to take its place.

In such a charge, there may be an element of truth; possibly there was a time in education when memory was over-estimated and thinking was deprived of its rights. But if the education of the past was one-sided in its emphasis upon acquaintance with facts, surely the pendulum has now swung to an opposite extreme which is more disastrous still. It is a travesty upon our pedagogic method when we are represented as regarding a mere storing up of lectures in the mind of the student as an end in itself. In point of fact, we regard it as a means to an end, but a very necessary means; we regard it not as a substitute for independent thinking, but as a necessary prerequisite for it. The student who accepts what we say without criticism and without thinking of his own is no doubt very unsatisfactory; but equally unsatisfactory is the student who undertakes to criticize what he knows nothing whatever about. Thinking cannot be carried on without the materials of thought; and the materials of thought are facts, or else assertions that are presented as facts. A mass of details stored up in the mind does not in itself make a thinker; but on the other hand thinking is absolutely impossible without that mass of details. And it is just this latter impossible operation of thinking without the materials of thought which is being advocated by modern pedagogy and is being put into practice only too well by modern students. In the presence of this tendency, we believe that facts and hard work ought again to be allowed to come to their rights: it is impossible to think with an empty mind.

If the growth of ignorance is lamentable in secular education, it is tenfold worse in the sphere of the Christian religion and in the sphere of the Bible. Bible classes today often avoid a study of the actual contents of the Bible as they would avoid pestilence or disease; to many persons in the Church the notion of getting the simple historical contents of the Bible straight in the mind is an entirely new idea.

When one is asked to preach at a church, the pastor sometimes asks the visiting preacher to conduct his Bible class, and sometimes he gives a hint as to how the class is ordinarily conducted. He makes it very practical, he says; he gives the class hints as to how to live during the following week. But when I for my part actually conduct such a class, I most emphatically do not give the members hints as to how to live during the following week. That is not because such hints are not useful, but because they are not all that is useful. It would be very sad if a Bible class did not get practical directions; but a class that gets nothing but practical directions is very poorly prepared for life. And so when I conduct the class I try to give them what they do not get on other occasions; I try to help them get straight in their minds the doctrinal and historical contents of the Christian religion.

The absence of doctrinal teaching and preaching is certainly one of the causes for the present lamentable ignorance in the Church. But a still more influential cause is found in the failure of the most important of all Christian educational institutions. The most important Christian educational institution is not the pulpit or the school, important as these institutions are; but it is the Christian family. And that institution has to a very large extent ceased to do its work. Where did those of us who have reached middle life really get our knowledge of the Bible? I suppose my experience is the same as that of a good many of us. I did not get my knowledge of the Bible from Sunday School or from any other school, but I got it on Sunday afternoons with my mother at home. And I will venture to say that although my mental ability was certainly of no extraordinary kind I had a better knowledge of the Bible at fourteen years of age than is possessed by many students in the theological Seminaries of the present day. Theological students come for the most part from Christian homes; indeed in very considerable proportion they are children of the manse. Yet when they have finished college and enter the theological Seminary many of them are quite ignorant of the simple contents of the English Bible.

The sad thing is that it is not chiefly the students' fault. These students, many of them, are sons of ministers; and by their deficiencies they reveal the fact that the ministers of the present day are not only substituting exhortation for instruction, ethics for theology, in their preaching; but are even neglecting the education of their own children. The lamentable fact is that the Christian home, as an educational institution, has largely ceased to function.

Certainly that fact serves to explain to a considerable extent the growth of ignorance in the Church. But the explanation itself requires an explanation; so far we have only succeeded in pushing the problem farther back. The ignorance of the Church is explained by the failure of the Christian family as an educational institution; but what in turn explains that failure? Why is it that Christian parents have neglected the instruction of their children; why is it that preaching has ceased to be educational and doctrinal; why is it that even Sunday Schools and Bible classes have come to consider solely applications of Christianity without studying the Christianity that is to be applied?[1] These questions take us into the very heart of the situation; the growth of ignorance in the Church, the growth of indifference with regard to the simple facts recorded in the Bible, all goes back to a great spiritual movement, really skeptical in its tendency, which has been going forward during the last one hundred years—a movement which appears not only in philosophers and theologians such as Kant and Schleiermacher and Ritschl, but also in a widespread attitude of plain men and women throughout the world. The depreciation of the intellect, with the exaltation in the place of it of the feelings or of the will, is, we think, a basic fact in modern life, which is rapidly leading to a condition in which men neither know anything nor care anything about the doctrinal content of the Christian religion, and in which there is in general a lamentable intellectual decline.

This intellectual decline is certainly not appearing exclusively among persons who are trying to be evangelical in their views about the Bible; but it is at least equally manifest among those who hold the opposing view. A striking feature of recent religious literature is the abandonment of scientific historical method even

---

[1] For a salutary insistence upon the fact that if we are to have applied Christianity, we must also have "a Christianity to apply," see Francis Shunk Downs, "Christianity and Today," in *Princeton Theological Review*, xx, 1922, pp. 287-304.

among those who regard themselves as in the van of scientific progress.

Scientific historical method in the interpretation of the Bible requires that the Biblical writers should be allowed to speak for themselves. A generation or so ago that feature of scientific method was exalted to the dignity of a principle, and was honored by a long name. It was called "grammatico-historical exegesis." The fundamental notion of it was that the modern student should distinguish sharply between what he would have said or what he would have liked to have the Biblical writer say, and what the writer actually did say. The latter question only was regarded as forming the subject-matter of exegesis.

This principle, in America at least, is rapidly being abandoned. It is not, indeed, being abandoned in theory; lip-service is still being paid to it. But it is being abandoned in fact. It is being abandoned by the most eminent scholars.

It is abandoned by Professor Goodspeed, for example, when in his translation of the New Testament he translates the Greek word meaning "justify," in important passages, by "make upright."[2] I confess that it is not without regret that I should see the doctrine of justification by faith, which is the foundation of evangelical liberty, thus removed from the New Testament; it is not without regret that I should abandon the whole of the Reformation and return with Professor Goodspeed to the merit-religion of the Middle Ages. But the

---

[2] Goodspeed, *The New Testament: An American Translation*, 1923.

point that I am now making is not that Professor Goodspeed's translation is unfortunate because it involves—as it certainly does—religious retrogression, but because it involves an abandonment of historical method in exegesis. It may well be that this question how a sinful man may become right with God does not interest the modern translator; but every true historian must certainly admit that it did interest the Apostle Paul. And the translator of Paul must, if he be true to his trust, place the emphasis where Paul placed it, and not where the translator could have wished it placed.

What is true in the case of Paul is also true in the case of Jesus. Modern writers have abandoned the historical method of approach. They persist in confusing the question what they could have wished that Jesus had been with the question what Jesus actually was. In reading one of the most popular recent books on the subject of religion, I came upon the following amazing assertion. "Jesus," the author says, "concerned himself but little with the question of existence after death."[8] In the presence of such assertions any student of history may well stand aghast. It may be that we do not make much of the doctrine of a future life, but the question whether Jesus did so is not a matter of taste but an historical question, which can be answered only on the basis of an examination of the sources of historical information that we call the Gospels.

And the result of such examination is perfectly plain. As a matter of fact, not only the thought of heaven but also the thought of hell runs all through the teaching

[8] Ellwood, *The Reconstruction of Religion*, 1922, p. 141.

of Jesus. It appears in all four of the Gospels; it appears in the sources, supposed to underlie the Gospels, which have been reconstructed, rightly or wrongly, by modern criticism. It imparts to the ethical teaching its peculiar earnestness. It is not an element which can be removed by any critical process, but simply suffuses the whole of Jesus' teaching and Jesus' life. "And fear not them which kill the body, but are not able to kill the soul: but rather fear him which is able to destroy both soul and body in hell."[4] "It is better for thee to enter into life with one eye, rather than having two eyes to be cast into hell fire"[5]—these words are not an excrescence in Jesus' teaching but are quite at the centre of the whole.

At any rate, if you are going to remove the thought of a future life from the teaching of Jesus, if at this point you are going to reject the *prima facie* evidence, surely you should do so only by a critical grounding of your procedure. And my point is that that critical grounding is now thought to be quite unnecessary. Modern American writers simply attribute their own predilections to Jesus without, apparently, the slightest scrutiny of the facts.

As over against this anti-intellectual tendency in the modern world, it will be one chief purpose of the present little book to defend the primacy of the intellect, and in particular to try to break down the false and disastrous opposition which has been set up between knowledge and faith.

[4] Matt. x: 28.
[5] Matt. xviii: 9.

No doubt it is unfortunate, if our theme be the intellect, that the writer has so very limited an experimental acquaintance with the subject that he is undertaking to discuss. But in these days the intellect cannot afford to be too critical of her defenders, since her defenders are few enough. Time was when reason sat in regal state upon her throne, and crowds of obsequious courtiers did her reverence. But now the queen has been deposed, and pragmatism the usurper occupies the throne. Some humble retainers still follow the exile of the fallen queen; some men still hope for the day of restoration when the useful will be relegated to its proper place and truth will again rule the world. But such retainers are few—so few that even the very humblest of them may perhaps out of charity be granted a hearing which in reason's better days he could not have claimed.

The attack upon the intellect has assumed many forms, and has received an elaborate philosophical grounding. With that philosophical grounding I am not so presumptuous as to attempt to deal. I am not altogether unaware of the difficulties that beset what may be called the common-sense view of truth; epistemology presents many interesting problems and some puzzling antinomies. But the antinomies of epistemology are like other antinomies which puzzle the human mind; they indicate the limitations of our intellect, but they do not prove that the intellect is not reliable so far as it goes. I for my part at least am not ready to give up the struggle; I am not ready to rest in a pragmatist skepticism; I am not ready to say that truth can never be attained.

But what are some of the ways in which the intellect, in the modern religious world, has been dethroned, or at least has been debarred from the sphere of ultimate reality?

In the first place, and most obviously, there is the distinction between religion and theology. Theology, it is said, is merely the necessarily changing expression of a unitary experience; doctrine can never be permanent, but is simply the clothing of religious experience in the forms of thought suitable to any particular generation. Those who speak in this way protest, indeed, that they are not seeking to do without theology, but are merely endeavoring to keep theology in its proper place. Theology, it is admitted, is necessary to religion; there can never be religion without some theology; but what particular theology it shall be, they hold, depends upon the habits of thought that prevail in the age in which the theology is produced.

In accordance with this principle, various creeds have recently been produced to take the place of the great historic confessions of faith—various creeds intended to "interpret" Christianity in the "thought-forms" of the twentieth century and to provide a basis for Christian unity. It is perfectly obvious that these modern formulations differ from those that they are intended to supplant in many important ways. But the most important difference of all has sometimes escaped notice. The most important difference is not that these modern creeds differ from the historic creeds in this

point or that; but it is that the historic creeds, unlike
the modern creeds, were intended by their authors or
compilers to be true. And I for my part believe that
that is the most necessary qualification of a creed. I
cannot, therefore, accept the protestations of those pragmatists who maintain that they are not hostile to theology. For if theology is not even intended to be permanently and objectively true, if it is merely a convenient symbol in which in this generation a mystic
experience is clothed, then theologizing, it seems to me,
is the most useless form of trifling in which a man
could possibly engage.

Certainly this theologizing of the pragmatist is as
far as possible removed from the kind of progress that
is found in the advance of science. The scientist does
indeed modify his opinions; one hypothesis often gives
place to another which is intended to be a better explanation of the facts. But the point is that the new hypothesis, like the old, is intended at least to be permanently correct: it *may* have to give way to a better
understanding of the facts, but there is nothing in the
very nature of the case to show that it *must* give way.
Science, in other words, though it may not in any
generation attain truth, is at any rate aiming at truth.

Very different is the activity of the pragmatist theologian. The pragmatist theologian, unlike the scientist, does not even intend his own formulations to be
permanent, but regards them as merely symbolic ex-
pressions, in the thought-forms of one particular generation, of an ineffable experience. According to the
pragmatist it is not merely inevitable that the theology

of one generation should differ from the theology of another, but it is desirable that it should do so. That theology, according to the pragmatist, is the best which most perfectly expresses the experience of religion in the "thought-forms" of any particular age. Thus the Nicene Creed, it is said, was admirable in the fourth century of our era, and the Westminster Confession was admirable in the seventeenth century, but these formulations must of course now give place to twentieth-century statements which so far as the literal or intellectual meaning is concerned are contradictory to them. Theology in other words is not to be judged in accordance with the degree of approximation which it attains to an eternally persisting norm of truth, but it is to be regarded as good or bad according as it serves the purposes of mankind and promotes an abundance of life.

Indeed this pragmatist attitude toward difference in theology is applied not only to successive generations, but also to simultaneously existing nations and races. It is unreasonable, some advocates of missions are accustomed to say, for missionaries to ask Eastern races to accept Western creeds; the Eastern mind cannot be forced into a Western mould; on the contrary, the East must be allowed to give its own expression to the Christian faith. And so sometimes we read more or less formal expositions of belief that have come from the native churches of the East. What an interesting thing the formation of such expositions is, to be sure! A fresh, new expression of the Christian religion independent of all the conventions of the West! Unfortunately such expectations are often sadly disappointed when one reads the new formulations for himself; the vaunted freshness and originality is often not to be seen, and what we actually have is a most unoriginal repetition of the vague naturalism of the contemporary Western world. The Eastern mind has turned out to be as like as two peas to the mind of the South Side of Chicago; all the stock phrases of modern agnosticism seem to be thoroughly acceptable to the Oriental students to whom they have been taught.

But if the results of these little experiments of the Eastern mind hardly seem to bear out the contention of the pragmatist—hardly seem to bear out the contention that the Eastern mind and the Western mind are so distinct that the thought-forms that suit one will not suit the other—the contention itself is thoroughly typical of our age; it is only one manifestation of a pragmatism that is all-pervasive. And that pragmatism involves the most bottomless skepticism which could possibly be conceived. According to the logic of the pragmatist position two contradictory doctrines may be equally good; for doctrine, in the opinion of the pragmatists, is merely the symbolic expression of an experience really inexpressible, and must necessarily change as the generations pass. There is, in other words, according to that view, no possibility that anything in the sphere of doctrine can be permanently and universally true.

Such a view of doctrinal changes is sometimes compared, as we have already hinted, to the progress of science; it is unreasonable, the pragmatist theologian says, to reject the physics and chemistry of the first

century or the seventeenth century and yet maintain
unchanged the theology of those past ages; why should
theology be exempt from the universal law of progress?

But this comparison, as indeed should be plain from
what has already been said, really involves a very
strange misconception; far from advocating progress in
theology, the current pragmatism really destroys the
very possibility of progress. For progress involves something to progress *to* as well as something to progress
from. And in the intellectual sphere the current pragmatism can find no goal of progress in an objective
norm of truth; one doctrine, according to the pragmatist view, may be just as good as an exactly contradictory doctrine, provided it suits a particular generation or a particular group of persons. The changes in
scientific hypotheses represent true progress because they
are increasingly close approximations to an objectively
and externally existent body of facts; while the changes
advocated by pragmatist theologians are not progress
at all but the meaningless changes of a kaleidoscope.

As over against this pragmatist attitude, we believers
in historic Christianity maintain the objectivity of
truth; and in doing so we and not the Modernists become advocates of progress. Theology, we hold, is
not an attempt to express in merely symbolic terms an
inner experience which must be expressed in different
terms in subsequent generations; but it is a setting forth
of those facts upon which experience is based. It is
not indeed a complete setting forth of those facts, and
therefore progress in theology become possible; but it
may be true so far as it goes; and only because there

is that possibility of attaining truth and of setting it
forth ever more completely can there be progress. Theology, in other words, is just as much a science as is
chemistry; and like the science of chemistry it is capable
of advance. The two sciences, it is true, differ widely
in their subject matter; they differ widely in the character of the evidence upon which their conclusions are
based; in particular they differ widely in the qualifications required of the investigator: but they are both
sciences, because they are both concerned with the acquisition and orderly arrangement of a body of truth.

At this point, then, we find the really important
divergence of opinion in the religious world at the
present day; the difference of attitude toward theology
or toward doctrine goes far deeper than any mere divergence in detail. The modern depreciation of theology results logically in the most complete skepticism.
It is not merely that the ancient creeds, and the Bible
upon which they are based, are criticized—indeed we
ourselves certainly think that they ought constantly to
be criticized in order that it may be seen that they will
stand the test—but the really serious trouble is that the
modern pragmatist, on account of the very nature of
his philosophy, has nothing to put in their place. The
ology, according to him, may be useful; but it can never
by any possibility be true. As Dr. Fosdick observes,
the liberalism of today must necessarily produce an intellectual formulation which will become the orthodoxy
of tomorrow, and which will then in turn have to
give place to a new liberalism; and so on (we sup-

pose) *ad infinitum*.[6]   This is what the plain man in
the Church has difficulty in understanding; he does not
yet appreciate the real gravity of the issue.   He does
not see that it makes very little difference how much
or how little of the creeds of the Church the Modernist
preacher affirms, or how much or how little of the
Biblical teaching from which the creeds are derived.
He might affirm every jot and tittle of the Westminster
Confession, for example, and yet be separated by a
great gulf from the Reformed Faith.   It is not that part
is denied and the rest affirmed; but all is denied, because
all is affirmed merely as useful or symbolic and not as
true.

Thus it comes about that to the believer in historic
Christianity the Modernist preacher is often most distressing just when he desires to be most concessive.   He
has no desire, he says, to combat the faith of simple
people in the Church; indeed the older "interpretations," he says, may be best for some people even now.
Such assertions are perhaps intended to be concessive;
but in reality they are to the believer in historic Christianity the most radically destructive assertions that
could possibly be made.   It would from our point of
view be better if the preacher, convinced of the falsity
of supernatural religion in the sense of the New Testament and of the creeds, became an apostle with the
courage of his convictions, and sought to root out of
every one's mind convictions that he holds to be false.
In that case we should indeed differ from him radically,

[6] Fosdick, *The Modern Use of the Bible*, 1924, p. 190.   **Compare** *Princeton Theological Review*, **xxiii**, 1925, p. 73.

but there would be at least a common ground for discussion. But the assertion that the historic creeds may
still be best for some people and the modern interpretations better for others, or the provision in plans of
Church union that the constituent churches should
recognize each the other's creed as valid for the other
church's members—this, we think, involves a sin
against the light of reason itself; and if the light that
is in us be darkness, how great is that darkness! A
thing that is useful may be useful for some and not for
others, but a thing that is true remains true for all
people and beyond the end of time.

But if theology be thus abandoned, or rather if (to
ease the transition) it be made merely the symbolic
expression of religious experience, what is to be put in
its place? Two answers to this question may perhaps
be distinguished in the religious life of the present day.
In the first place, there is mysticism; and in the second
place, there is a kind of neo-positivism.

Mysticism unquestionably is the natural result of the
anti-intellectual tendency which now prevails; for
mysticism is the consistent exaltation of experience at
the expense of thought. But in actual practice mysticism is seldom consistent; indeed it cannot possibly be
consistent if it seeks to explain itself to the world.
The experience upon which it is based, or in which it
consists, is said to be ineffable; yet mystics love to talk
about that experience all the same. Dr. E. S. Waterhouse[7] quotes an epigram of Mr. Bradley "to the effect
that Herbert Spencer told us more about the Unknow-

7 *Philosophy of Religious Experience*, 1923, pp. 201 f.

able than the rashest of theologians has told us about God." So it may perhaps be said that mystics are accustomed to express the inexpressible more fully than the ineffable character which they attribute to their experience may seem to warrant.

In particular, those who discard theology in the interests of experience are inclined to make use of a personal way of talking and thinking about God to which they have no right. A noted preacher, for example, relates an incident of his youth in which he overheard his father praying when he thought that he was alone with God. His father, says the preacher, was thoroughly orthodox, and devoted to the Westminster Shorter Catechism. Yet in that prayer, to the amazement of the boy, there was none of the elaborate theology of the Westminster Standards, but only a simple outpouring of the soul in the presence of God. "It was a prayer," says the preacher, "in which he threw himself into the arms of his heavenly Father. There was in it no theology, no hell, no moral or substitutionary theory of the atonement."

But what was it after all that caused that simple outpouring of the soul? Was that prayer so independent of theology as the preacher seems to think? For our part we doubt it very much. All personal communion seems to be a simple thing; yet it is in reality very complex. My friendship for a human friend, for example, depends upon years of observation of my friend's actions. So it is exactly in the case of the communion of the Christian with his God. The Christian says: "Lord, thou knowest that we are on the same old terms." It seems very simple and very unthcological. But in reality it depends upon the whole rich content of God's revelation of Himself in the salvation which He has provided through His Son. At any rate, pure feeling, if it ever exists, is non-moral; what makes our relation to another person, whether a human friend or the eternal God, such an ennobling thing is the knowledge which we have of the character of that person. The experience of the real mystic, then, as distinguished from that experience of direct contact with God in the depths of the soul which is popularly called mysticism—the latter being of course a part of all vital religion—is not Christian experience; for Christian experience is a thoroughly personal thing; the Christian holds fellowship with a Person whom he knows.

Another substitute for a religion based upon the knowledge of God is positivism. The name itself is due to a phenomenon that appeared long ago, but the thing that the name represents has in all essentials been revived. It has been revived in rather definite fashion, for example, by Professor Ellwood in his popular book, *The Reconstruction of Religion*. Professor Ellwood himself detects his affinity for the older positivism, though he seeks to supplement the positivist religion of humanity with a pantheizing reverence for the world-process. But positivism has also been revived, though often unconsciously, by those popular preachers of the day who use the phrase, the "Christlike God," which is so distressing to men who have thought at all deeply upon the things at the basis of Christian faith—by those

popular preachers who tell us that God is known
only through Jesus.   If they meant that God is known
only through the Second Person of the Trinity, the
eternal Logos, I might perhaps agree; and for my agreement I might perhaps find warrant in the eleventh chapter of Matthew.   But of course as a matter of fact that is
not at all what they mean.   What they mean is that all
metaphysics having been abandoned or relegated to the
realm of unessential speculation—all questions as to
whether there is a God who made the world by the fiat
of His will, or whether there is a life after death, or
whether Jesus in very person is living today—all such
questions having been abandoned, the soul of man may
be transformed by the mere contemplation and emula-
tion of the moral life of Jesus.   Essentially, such a religion is positivism; it regards as non-essential all extra-
mundane factors and sets up a religion of humanity—a
religion of humanity symbolized by the name of Jesus.

Certainly the Jesus to whom such a religion can appeal
is not the Jesus of history—neither the Jesus set forth
in the New Testament nor the Jesus who has been reproduced, or ever conceivably can be reproduced, by any
critical process.   For the real Jesus certainly was a theist,
certainly did believe in a really existent God, Maker of
the world and final Judge, certainly did accept the revelation of God in the Old Testament Scriptures, certainly
did place the doctrine of heaven and hell at the very
foundation of His ethical teaching, certainly did look
for a catastrophic coming of the Kingdom of God.
These things in much modern preaching are ignored.
The preacher quotes some word of Jesus quite out of its

context—perhaps even from the Gospel of John, which
the preacher's own critical principles have discarded—
and then proceeds to derive from that misunderstood
word of Jesus a non-doctrinal religion of this world.
Some of us, as we listen, may desire to ask questions.
Some of us may desire to ask whether Jesus of Nazareth
really made the more abundant life of man the ultimate
end of existence; some of us may desire to ask whether
Jesus really left His own person out of His gospel and
whether we can really reject, on any critical principles,
those words of His in which He claimed to be the Judge
of the whole earth.   But such questions receive short
shrift from the Modernist preacher; they involve, he
says, merely evasions, on our part, of the moral demands
of Jesus.   At no point does the passionate anti-intellectualism of the Modernist Church appear more clearly
than here.

But can the human reason, especially as manifested
in the historical sense, really be thus browbeaten into
silence?   For our part, we do not believe that it can.
And when the reason awakes, though the modern religion of humanity may conceivably remain, its appeal
to Jesus of Nazareth at least will have to go.   We shall
have to cease investing our pride in human goodness
with the borrowed trappings of Christianity's emotional appeal; and the choice will have to be made between abandonment of Jesus as the moral guide of the
race and acceptance of His stupendous claims.

Thus the relinquishment of theology in the interests
of non-doctrinal religion really involves the relinquishment of Christianity in the interests of a skepticism than

which a more complete could scarcely be conceived. But
another contrast has an equally baleful effect upon the
life of the present day.   It is the contrast between
knowledge and faith; and the consideration of that contrast takes us into the heart of our present subject. That
contrast, as we shall see, ignores an essential element in
faith; and what is called faith after the subtraction of
that element is not faith at all.   As a matter of fact all
true faith involves an intellectual element; all faith involves knowledge and issues in knowledge.

The exhibition of that fact will form a considerable
part of the discussion that follows. It will not, indeed,
form all of it; since the discussion will not be merely
polemic; but after all the only way to get a clear idea
of what a thing is, is to place it in contrast with what
it is not; all definition involves exclusion. We shall
endeavor, therefore, by comparison of opposing views,
as well as by exhibition of our own, to arrive at an
answer to the question, "What is Faith?"   If that
question were rightly answered, the Church, we believe,
would soon emerge from its present perplexities and
would go forth with a new joy to the conquest of the
world.

There are those who shrink from a consideration of
these great questions of principle; there are those who
decry controversy, and believe that the Church should
return to its former policy of politely ignoring or taking
for granted the central things of the Christian faith.
But with such persons I, for my part, cannot possibly
bring myself to agree.   The period of apparent harmony in which the Church in America found itself

a few years ago was, I believe, a period of the deadliest peril; loyalty to Church organizations was being substituted for loyalty to Christ; Church leaders who never even mentioned the centre of the gospel in their preaching were in undisputed charge of the resources of the Church; at board meetings or in the councils of the Church, it was considered bad form even to mention, at least in any definite and intelligible way, the Cross of Christ. A polite paganism, in other words, with reliance upon human resources, was being quietly and peacefully substituted for the heroism of devotion to the gospel.

In the face of such a condition, there were some men whose hearts were touched; the Lord Jesus had died for them upon the cross, and the least they could do, they thought, was to be faithful to Him; they could not continue to support, by their gifts and by their efforts, anything that was hostile to His gospel; and they were compelled, therefore, in the face of all opposition, to raise the question what it is that the Church is in the world to do.

God grant that question may never be silenced until it is answered aright! Let us not fear the opposition of men; every great movement in the Church from Paul down to modern times has been criticized on the ground that it promoted censoriousness and intolerance and disputing. Of course the gospel of Christ, in a world of sin and doubt, will cause disputing; and if it does not cause disputing and arouse bitter opposition, that is a fairly sure sign that it is not being faithfully proclaimed. As for me, I believe that a great opportunity has been opened to Christian people by the "contro-versy" that is so much decried.   Conventions have been broken down; men are trying to penetrate beneath pious words to the thing that these words designate; it is becoming increasingly necessary for a man to choose whether he will stand with Christ or against Him. Such a condition, I for my part believe, has been brought about by the Spirit of God; already there has been gen-uine spiritual advance.   It has been signally manifested at the institution which I have the honor to serve.   The morale of our theological student body during the past years had been becoming rather low; there was marked indifference to the central things of the faith; and re-ligious experience was of the most superficial kind. But during the academic year, 1924-1925, there has been something like an awakening. Youth has begun to think for itself; the evil of compromising associations has been discovered; Christian heroism in the face of opposi-tion has come again to its rights; a new interest has been aroused in the historical and philosophical questions that underlie the Christian religion; true and independent convictions have been formed.   Controversy, in other words, has resulted in a striking intellectual and spiritual advance. Some of us discern in all this the work of the Spirit of God. And God grant that His fire be not quenched!   God save us from any smoothing over of these questions in the interests of a hollow pleasantness; God grant that great questions of principle may never rest until they are settled right! It is out of such times of questioning that great revivals come.   God grant that it may be so today!   Controversy of the right sort is good; for out of such controversy, as Church history and Scripture alike teach, there comes the salvation of souls.

It is with such an ultimate aim that we consider the question, "What is Faith?" A more "practical" question could hardly be conceived. The preacher says: "Believe on the Lord Jesus Christ, and thou shall be saved." But how can a man possibly act on that suggestion, unless he knows what it is to believe. It was at that point that the "doctrinal" preaching of a former generation was far more practical than the "practical" preaching of the present day. I shall never forget the pastor of the church in which I grew up. He was a good preacher in many ways, but his most marked characteristic was the plainness and definiteness with which he told the people what a man should do to be saved. The preachers of the present time allude to the importance of becoming a Christian, but they seldom seem to make the matter the subject of express exposition; they leave the people with a vague impression to the effect that being a Christian is a good thing, but this impression is difficult to translate into action because definite directions are absent. These preachers speak about faith, but they do not tell what faith is.

It is to help in some small way to supply this lack that the present little book has been written. If the way of salvation is faith, it does seem to be highly important to tell people who want to be saved just what faith means. If a preacher cannot do that, he can hardly be a true evangelist.

How, then, shall we obtain the answer to our question; how shall we discover what faith is?   At first sight it might seem to be a purely philosophical or perhaps psychological question; there is faith other than faith in Jesus Christ; and such faith no doubt is to be included with Christian faith in the same general category.   It looks, therefore, as though I were engaging upon a psychological discussion, and as though I ought to be thoroughly familiar with the epistemological and psychological questions that are involved.

Undoubtedly such a treatment of the subject would be highly useful and instructive; but unfortunately I am not competent to undertake it.   I propose therefore a somewhat different method of approach.   How would it be if we should study the subject of faith, not so much by generalizations from various instances of faith in human life (though such generalizations will not be altogether absent), but rather by a consideration of faith as it appears in its highest and plainest manifestation? Such concentration upon a classic example is often the best possible way, or at any rate one very fruitful way, in which a subject can be treated.

But the classic example of faith is to be found in the faith that is enjoined in the New Testament.   I think that there will be widespread agreement with that assertion among students of psychology whether Christian or not; the insistence upon faith is characteristic of New Testament Christianity; there is some justification, surely, for the way in which Paul speaks of the pre-Christian period as the time "before faith came."   No doubt that assertion is intended by the Apostle as relative merely; he himself insists that faith had a place in the old dispensation; but such anticipations were swallowed up, by the coming of Christ, in a glorious fulfilment. At any rate, the Bible as a whole, taking prophecy and fulfilment together, is the supreme textbook on the subject of faith.   The study of that textbook may lead to as clear an understanding of our subject as could be attained by any more general investigation; we can learn what faith is best of all by studying it in its highest manifestation.   We shall ask, then, in the following chapters what the Bible, and in particular the New Testament, tells us about faith.

CHAPTER II

FAITH IN GOD

In the first place, the Bible certainly tells us that faith involves a person as its object. We can indeed speak about having faith in an impersonal object, such as a machine, but when we do so I think we are indulging in a sort of personification of that object, or else we are really thinking about the men who made the machine. At any rate, without discussing the correctness or incorrectness of this usage, we can at least say that such a use of the word stops short of the highest significance. In the highest significance of the word—the significance in which alone we are now interested—faith is regarded as being always reposed in persons.

The Persons in whom according to the Bible faith is particularly to be reposed are God the Father and the Lord Jesus Christ.

But—and here we come to the point which we think ought to be emphasized above all others just at the present day—it is impossible to have faith in a person without having knowledge of the person; far from being contrasted with knowledge, faith is founded upon knowledge. That assertion runs counter to the whole trend of contemporary religious teaching; but a little reflection, I think, will show that it is indubitably correct, and that it must be applied specifically to the objects of Christian faith. Let us consider from this point of view first faith in God and second faith in Jesus Christ.

In the classic treatment of faith in the Epistle to the Hebrews, there is a verse that goes to the very root of the matter. "He that cometh to God," the author says, "must believe that he is, and that he is a rewarder of them that diligently seek him."[1] Here we find a rejection in advance of all the pragmatist, non-doctrinal Christianity of modern times.

In the first place, religion is here made to depend absolutely upon doctrine; the one who comes to God must not only believe *in* a person, but he must also believe *that* something is true; faith is here declared to involve acceptance of a proposition. There could be no plainer insistence upon the doctrinal or intellectual basis of faith. It is impossible, according to the Epistle to the Hebrews, to have faith in a person without accepting with the mind the facts about the person.

Entirely different is the prevailing attitude in the modern Church; far from recognizing, as the author of Hebrews does, the intellectual basis of faith, many modern preachers set faith in sharp opposition to knowledge. Christian faith, they say, is not assent to a creed, but it is confidence in a person. The Epistle to the Hebrews on the other hand declares that it is impossible to have confidence in a person without assenting to a creed. "He that cometh to God must believe that he is." The words, "God is," or "God exists," constitute a creed; they constitute a proposition; and yet they are here placed as necessary to that supposedly non-intellectual thing that is called faith. It would be impossible to

[1] Heb. xi: 6.

find a more complete opposition than that which here appears between the New Testament and the anti-intellectualistic tendency of modern preaching.

But here as elsewhere the Bible is found to be true to the plainest facts of the soul; whereas the modern separation between faith in a person and acceptance of a creed is found to be psychologically false. It is perfectly true, of course, that faith in a person is more than acceptance of a creed, but the Bible is quite right in holding that it always involves acceptance of a creed. Confidence in a person is more than intellectual assent to a series of propositions about the person, but it always involves those propositions, and becomes impossible the moment they are denied. It is quite impossible to trust a person about whom one assents to propositions that make the person untrustworthy, or fails to assent to propositions that make him trustworthy. Assent to certain propositions is not the whole of faith, but it is an absolutely necessary element in faith. So assent to certain propositions about God is not all of faith in God, but it is necessary to faith in God; and Christian faith, in particular, though it is more than assent to a creed, is absolutely impossible without assent to a creed. One cannot trust a God whom one holds with the mind to be either non-existent or untrustworthy.

The Epistle to the Hebrews, therefore, is quite right in maintaining that "he that cometh to God must believe that he is." In order to trust God or to have communion with Him we must at least believe that He exists.

At first sight that might seem to be a mere truism;
it might seem to be something that every sane person
would be obliged to accept.   As a matter of fact, however, even this apparently self-evident proposition is rejected by a great mass of persons in the modern world;
and it has been rejected by many persons in the course
of religious history.   What the Epistle to the Hebrews
accomplishes by enunciating the simple proposition,
"He that cometh to God must believe that he is," is the
repudiation of that important phenomenon in the history of religion that is known as mysticism.

The true mystic holds that communion with God is
an ineffable experience, which is independent of any intellectual propositions whatever.   Religion, the mystic
holds, in its pure form is independent of the intellect;
when it is expressed in an intellectual mold it is cabined
and confined; such expression can be nothing more than
symbolic; religious experience itself does not depend upon assent to any kind of creed.   In opposition to this
mystical attitude the author of the Epistle to the Hebrews insists upon the primacy of the intellect; he bases
religion squarely upon truth.   He does not, of course,
reject that immediate and mysterious contact of the soul
with God which is dear to the mystic's heart; for that
immediate contact of the soul with God is a vital part
of all religion worthy of the name.   But he does break
down the mystical separation between that experience on
the one hand and the knowledge of God on the other;
and in doing so he is uttering not a truism but an important truth; he is delivering a salutary blow against
anti-intellectual mysticism ancient and modern.   There

could be, under present conditions, no more timely text; in the presence of this stupendous utterance, so far-reaching yet so simple, the non-doctrinal religion of the present day seems to be but a shallow and ephemeral thing.

It is not true, then, according to the New Testament, that religion is independent of doctrine or that faith is independent of knowledge; on the contrary, communion with God or faith in God is dependent upon the doctrine of His existence. But it is dependent upon other doctrines in addition to that. "He that cometh to God," says the Epistle to the Hebrews, "must believe that he is, *and that he is a rewarder of them that diligently seek him.*" In this latter part of the sentence, we have, expressed in a concrete way, the great truth of the personality of God. God, according to the Epistle to the Hebrews, is One who can act—act in view of a judgment upon those who come to Him. What we have here, in the second part of this sentence, is a presentation of what the Bible elsewhere calls the "living" God. God not only exists, but is a free Person who can act.

The same truth appears with even greater clearness in the third verse of the same great chapter. "Through faith we understand," says the author, "that the worlds were framed by the word of God, so that things which are seen were not made of things which do appear." Here we have, expressed with a clearness that leaves nothing to be desired, the doctrine of creation out of nothing, and that doctrine is said to be received by faith. It is the same doctrine that appears in the first verse of the Bible, "In the beginning God created the heaven and the earth," and that really is presupposed in the Bible from beginning to the end. Yet the prevalent religious tendency in the Church of the present day relegates that doctrine to the realm of the non-essential. "What has religion to do," we are asked, "with the obsolete notion of fiat creation?"

The truth is that in the Epistle to the Hebrews as well as in the rest of the Bible we are living in a world of thought that is diametrically opposed to the anti-intellectualism of the present day. Certain things, according to the Bible, are known about God, and without these things there can be no faith. To the pragmatist skepticism of the modern religious world, therefore, the Bible is sharply opposed; against the passionate anti-intellectualism of a large part of the modern Church it maintains the primacy of the intellect; it teaches plainly that God has given to man a faculty of reason which is capable of apprehending truth, even truth about God.

That does not mean that we finite creatures can find out God by our own searching; but it does mean that God has made us capable of receiving the information which He chooses to give. I cannot evolve an account of China out of my own inner consciousness, but I am perfectly capable of understanding the account which comes to me from travellers who have been there themselves. So our reason is certainly insufficient to tell us about God unless He reveals Himself; but it is capable (or would be capable if it were not clouded by sin) of receiving revelation when once it is given.

God's revelation of Himself to man embraces, indeed.

only a small part of His being; the area of what we
know is infinitesimal compared with the area of what
we do not know.   But partial knowledge is not necessarily false knowledge; and our knowledge of God
on the basis of His revelation of Himself is, we hold,
true as far as it goes.

That knowledge of God is regarded by the Bible as
involved in faith and as the necessary prerequisite of
faith.   We can trust God, according to the Bible, because He has revealed Himself as trustworthy.   The
knowledge that God has graciously given us of Himself
is the basis of our confidence in Him; the God of the
Bible is One whom it is reasonable to trust.

But that certainly cannot be said of the God who is
presented by much of modern speculation; there are
ways of thinking about God, widely prevalent today,
which will inevitably destroy our confidence in Him.

In the first place there is the widespread pantheism
of the day, which brings God into some sort of necessary connection with the world.   According to the pan-
theistic view, not only does the world not exist apart
from God, but God does not exist apart from the world;
God is either to be identified with the totality of the
world-process or else He is to be regarded as connected
with the world-process as the soul of man is connected
with his body.   That way of thinking is very widespread and very popular; it is called, by a perversion of
a great truth, the "immanence" of God; it runs through
a large part of contemporary preaching.   Whether explicit or not, whether thoroughgoing or present only in
tendency, pantheism colors very largely the religious life

of our time. Yet as a matter of fact it will ultimately make religious life impossible; certainly it will make impossible anything that can be called faith. It is really impossible to trust a being that is conceived of merely as the whole of which we are parts; in order to trust God one must think of God as a transcendent, living Person.

It is true that pantheists represent their view as bringing God near to man. "We will have nothing to do," they say in effect, "with the far-off God of the creeds of the Church; the problem of the union between God and man, with which the older theologians wrestled and as a solution of which they constructed their elaborate doctrine of redemption, is no problem at all for us; to us God is closer than breathing and nearer than hands and feet; His life pulses through the life of all the world and through the lives of every one of us." Thus pantheism is substituted for theism on the ground that it brings God nearer to men.

In reality, however, it has exactly the opposite effect. Far from bringing God nearer to man, the pantheism of our day really pushes Him very far off; it brings Him physically near, but at the same time makes Him spiritually remote; it conceives of Him as a sort of blind vital force, but ceases to regard Him as a Person whom a man can love and whom a man can trust. Destroy the free personality of God, and the possibility of fellowship with Him is gone; we cannot love or trust a God of whom we are parts.

Thus if we are going to retain faith we must cling with all our hearts to what are called the metaphysical attributes of God—His infinity and omnipotence and creatorhood. The finite God of Mr. H. G. Wells and of some other modern men, for example, seems to us to be almost as destructive of faith as is the impersonal God of the pantheists; He seems to us to be but a curious product of a modern mythology; He is not God but a god; and in the presence of all such imaginings we for our part are obliged to turn very humbly but very resolutely toward the dread, stupendous wonder of the infinite and say with Augustine: "Thou hast made us for Thyself, and our heart is restless until it finds its rest in Thee."

This devotion to the so-called metaphysical attributes of God is unpopular at the present day. There are many who tell us that we ought to cease to be interested in the question how the world was made, or what will be our fate when we pass beyond the grave; but that we can hold to the goodness of God though His creatorhood and His might are gone.

A notable presentation of such a view is found in Dr. McGiffert's book, *The God of the Early Christians*.[2] That book is very provocative and to our mind very erroneous. But it possesses at least one merit that is rare among contemporary religious literature—it is interesting. It is the work of one of the foremost American scholars, who is possessed of a radical, incisive mind, which, if it does not succeed in solving the problem of Christian origins, at least, unlike most contem-

---

[2] Arthur Cushman McGiffert, *The God of the Early Christians*, 1924. Compare for what follows the more extended treatment of the book in *The Princeton Theological Review*, xxii, 1924, pp. 544-588.

porary minds, detects what the problem is. Such a book, with its learning and its originality, whatever may be its faults, repays careful examination far more than many a five-foot shelf of the ostensibly startling and progressive but really thoroughly conventional religious books which are so popular just now.

Dr. McGiffert himself is an advocate of an "ethical theism," which is very far removed indeed from what the word "theism" can properly be held to mean. The question as to how the world came into being is, he holds, a matter of indifference to religion, as is the whole question of the power of God in the physical realm. But we moderns, he says in effect, though we are no longer interested in the power of God, can hold at least to our faith in goodness; and in doing so we can be religious men.

He is, however, far too good a scholar to suppose that this non-theistic "ethical theism" is taught in the New Testament; certainly, he admits, it was not taught by Jesus. Jesus' doctrine of God, on the contrary, he says, was nothing new; it was simply the Jewish doctrine which He found ready to hand; it laid great stress on the sovereignty of God, the absolute power of the Creator over His creatures, and it laid great stress upon the awful severity of God rather than upon His love. In other words, Dr. McGiffert admits—though his terminology is somewhat different—that Jesus was a "theist" in the usual meaning of that word; the whole sentimental picture of the "liberal Jesus," with his "practical" view of God that was not also theoretical, and with his one-sided emphasis upon the Fatherhood

of God as over against His justice, is here brushed resolutely aside.   Dr. McGiffert has read the Gospels for
himself, and knows full well how unhistorical that picture of Jesus is.

Paul, also, according to Dr. McGiffert, was a theist;
he maintained the Jewish view of God which Jesus
had taught, though he added to that view the worship
of Jesus as a Saviour God.   But—and here we come
to the really distinctive thesis of the book—the primitive simple-minded Gentile Christians in the early days,
unlike Jesus and unlike Paul, were, according to Dr.
McGiffert, not monotheists; they took Jesus as their
Saviour without being interested in denying the existence of other saviours; in particular they were not interested in the connection between Jesus and a Maker and
Ruler of the world.

The interesting thing about this remarkable theory
is not found in any likelihood of its truth, for it is not
really difficult to refute; but it is found in the connection between the theory and the whole anti-intellectualistic trend of the modern religious world.   Dr.
McGiffert, as most Modernists have done, has given up
any clear belief in theism; he has ceased to base his
religion upon a supreme Maker and Ruler of the
world: yet he desires to maintain some sort of continuity with the primitive Christian Church. And he does
so by the discovery of a primitive non-theistic[3] Gentile

---

[3] It is hoped that our readers will pardon our use of this hy-
brid word.   "Atheistic" obviously would not do at all.   And
even "antitheistic" would perhaps be too strong; since Dr. Mc-
Giffert does not maintain that these Christians expressly denied
theism, but only that they were not interested in it.

Christianity whose religion in important respects was similar to his own. The interesting thing about the book is not the thesis itself so much as the way in which in the propounding of the thesis the author's assumptions are allowed to appear.

The incorrectness of those assumptions becomes evident at many points. Particularly faulty is the separation of "salvation" from theism—a separation which recurs again and again in the book. "That there were philosophical thinkers," the author says, "who were attracted by the monotheism of the Jews and became Christians because of it is undoubtedly true, but they were vastly in the minority, and the Roman world was not won to Christianity by any such theological interest. On the contrary, faith in Christ and in his salvation converted the masses then, as it has converted multitudes in every age since."[4] It was therefore, according to the author, a decline—such is the clear implication of the book—when "Christianity ceased to be a mere religion of salvation—a mere saving cult—and Christ ceased to be a mere saviour;" when He became, instead, the "creator, ruler, and judge of all the earth."

This separation between theism and salvation ignores the simple fact that there can be no salvation without something from which a man is saved. If Christ saves the Christians, from what does He save them? Dr. McGiffert never seems to raise that question. But the answer to it is abundantly plain, and it destroys the entire reconstruction which this book so brilliantly attempts. Is it not abundantly plain that

[4] *Op. cit.,* pp. 44 f.

Christ saves Christians from sin, and from the consequences which it brings at the judgment-seat of God?
And is it not plain also that this was just the thing
that appealed most strongly to simple people of the
first century, as it appeals most strongly to many persons today? The truth is, it is quite impossible to
think of Christ as Saviour without thinking of the
thing from which He saves; the justice of God is everywhere the presupposition of the Saviourhood of Christ.
No doubt modern men, especially in the circles in which
Dr. McGiffert moves, have lost the sense of sin and
guilt and the fear of God's awful judgment-seat. But
with this loss there goes the general abandonment even
of the word "salvation," to say nothing of the idea.
Without the sense of sin and the fear of hell, there may
be the desire for improvement, "uplift," betterment;
but desire for "salvation," properly speaking, there cannot be. Modernism does not really "read Christianity
in terms of salvation," but reads salvation out of Christianity. It usually gives even the word "salvation"
up. For salvation presupposes something from which
a man is saved; it presupposes the awful wrath of a
righteous God; in other words it presupposes just the
thing which the non-theistic Modernism of Dr. Mc-
Giffert and others is most eager to reject. Very different was the situation in the early days of the Christian Church. Modern men have lost the sense of guilt
and the fear of hell, but the early Christians, whether
Jews or Gentiles, had not. They accepted Christ as
Saviour only because He could rescue them from the
abyss and bring them into right relation to the Ruler

and Judge of all the earth.   The Saviourhood of Christ
involved, then as always, the majesty and justice of
God.

Even more radically at fault is another distinction
which is at the very root of Dr. McGiffert's thinking
throughout—the distinction, already alluded to, "between a god of moral and a god of physical power."[5]
According to this distinction, Dr. McGiffert holds, as
we have already seen, that it is or should be matter of
indifference to Christians how the world came into
being; the doctrine of creation belongs, he thinks, to a
region of metaphysics with which religion need have
nothing to do.   Similar is really the case with respect
to the doctrine of providence; the whole thought of
the power, as distinguished from the goodness, of God
is, this author evidently thinks, quite separable from
religion; we can, he thinks, revere God's goodness without fearing His power or relying upon His protection
from physical ills.

Such skepticism may be justified or may not be justified—with that great question we shall not now undertake to deal—but indifferent to religion it certainly is
not.   Give up the thought of a Maker and Ruler of
the world; say, as you must logically say if you accept
Dr. McGiffert's view, that "the Great Companion is
dead," and you may still maintain something like religious fervor among a few philosophical souls.   But
the suffering mass of humanity, at any rate, will be lost
and hopeless in a hostile world.   And to represent
these things as matters of indifference to religion is to

---

[5] *Op. cit.*, p. 154.

close one's eyes to the deepest things of the human
heart. Is the doctrine of creation really a matter of
no religious moment; may the religious man really revere God without asking the question how the world
came into being and what it is that upholds it on its
way? Is the modern scientist wrong, who, pursuing
his researches into nature's laws, comes at length before
a curtain that is never lifted and stands in humble awe
before a mystery that rebukes all pride? Was Isaiah
wrong when he turned his eyes to the starry heavens
and said: "Lift up your eyes on high, and behold who
hath created these things, that bringeth out their host
by number: he calleth them all by names by the greatness of his might, for that he is strong in power; not
one faileth"? Was Jesus wrong when He bade His
disciples trust in Him who clothed the lilies of the field
and said: "Fear not, little flock; for it is your Father's
good pleasure to give you the kingdom?"

To these questions philosophers may return this
answer or that, but the answer of the Christian heart
at any rate is clear. "Away with all pale abstractions,"
it cries, "away with all dualism between the God of
power and the God of goodness, away with Marcion
and his many modern followers, away with those who
speak of the goodness of God but deprive Him of His
power. As for us Christians, we say still, as we contemplate that green field gleaming in the sun and those
dark forests touched with autumn brilliance and that
blue vault of heaven above—we say still, despite all,
that it is God's world, which He created by the fiat

of His will, and that through Christ's grace we are safe
forever in the arms of our heavenly Father."

But what have we left when, according to Dr. Mc-
Giffert, our heavenly Father is gone? The answer that
he gives is plain. "We have goodness left," we are told
in effect; "we do not know how the world came to
exist, we do not know what will be our fate when we
pass through the dark portals of death. But we can
find a higher, disinterested worship—far higher, it
would seem, than that of Jesus—in the reverence for
goodness divested of the vulgar trappings of power."

It sounds noble at first. But consider it for a moment, and its glory turns into ashes and leaves us in
despair. What is meant by a goodness that has no
physical power? Is not "goodness" in itself the merest
abstraction? Is it not altogether without meaning except as belonging to a person? And does not the very
notion of a person involve the power to act? Goodness altogether divorced from power is therefore no
goodness at all. And if it were goodness, it would still
mean nothing to us—included as we are in this physical
universe, which is capable apparently of destroying us
in its relentless march. The truth is that overmuch
abstraction has here destroyed even that which is intended to be conserved. Make God good only and not
powerful, and both God and goodness have really been
destroyed.

Feeling, even if not fully understanding, this objection, feeling that goodness is a mere empty abstraction
unless it inheres in good persons, many modern men
have tried to give their reverence for goodness some

sort of subsistence by symbolizing this "ethical" (and
most clearly antitheistic) "theism" in the person of
Jesus of Nazareth. They "read Christianity only in
terms of salvation" and take the man Jesus as their
only God. But who is this Jesus whom they make
the embodiment of the goodness that they revere? He
is certainly not the Jesus of the New Testament; for
that Jesus insisted upon everything that these modern
men reject. But he is not even the Jesus of modern
reconstruction; for even that Jesus, as Dr. McGiffert
has shown with devastating clearness, maintained the
theism which these modern men are rejecting with such
contempt. The truth is that it is impossible for such
men to hold to Jesus even as the supreme man, even
as the supreme embodiment of that abstract goodness
which Modernism is endeavoring to revere. For the
real Jesus placed at the very centre, not merely of His
thinking but of His life, the heavenly Father, Maker
and Ruler of the world.

Is, then, the antitheistic Modernism of our day, reading Christianity solely in terms of salvation and taking the man Jesus as its only God, to relinquish all
thought of continuity with the early glories of the
Christian Church? Here Dr. McGiffert comes with a
suggestion of hope. He abandons, indeed, the former
answers to the question; he destroys without pity the
complacency of those who have supposed that the early
history of Christianity on naturalistic principles is all
perfectly settled and plain; he throws the historical
problem again into a state of flux. Hence we welcome
his brilliant and thought-provoking book. Such books,

we believe, by their very radicalism, by their endeavor after ever new hypotheses, by the exhibition which they afford of the failure of all naturalistic reconstructions—especially their own—may ultimately lead to an abandonment of the whole weary effort, and a return to the simple grounding of Christian history upon a supernatural act of God. Meanwhile, however, Dr. McGiffert comes to the Modernist Church with a word of cheer. The continuity with primitive Christianity, he says in effect, does not need to be given up even by an antitheistic, non-theological Christianity which at first sight seems very non-primitive indeed.

It would be a great mistake, we think, to ignore this practical reference of the book. It is no doubt largely unconscious; Dr. McGiffert writes no doubt with the most earnest effort after scientific objectivity. But no historian can be altogether without presuppositions; and the presupposition of this historian is that an non-theistic Christianity is the most natural thing in the world. Accordingly, as many notable historians have done, he finds what he expects to find. Baur, on the basis of his Hegelian philosophy, with its "thesis, antithesis, synthesis," expected to find a conflict in the apostolic age with a gradual compromise and settlement. And so he found that phenomenon surely enough—in defiance of the facts, but in agreement with his philosophy. Similarly Dr. McGiffert, on the basis of his pragmatist skepticism, expects to find somewhere in the early Church a type of religious life s milar to his own.

Why is it that despite this author s own admission of the precariousness of many of his arguments he yet

"cannot resist the conclusion that there was such a primitive Christianity" as that which he has just described?[6]
The answer is plain. It is because he is seeking a precursor in early Christianity for the non-theistic Modernism which he himself supports. Others have found
precursors for it in the New Testament—even in Paul.
But Dr. McGiffert is far too good a scholar to be satisfied with any such solution as that. Still others have
found it in Jesus, and so have raised the cry, "Back to
Christ." But Dr. McGiffert has read the Gospels for
himself, and knows full well how false is that appeal
of the popular Modernist preachers to the words of the
one whom they call "Master." Rejecting these obviously false appeals, this author is obliged to find what
he seeks in the non-literary, inarticulate, and indeed
unattested, piety of the early Gentile Christians.
"There," he says in effect to his fellow-Modernists, "is
our religion at last; there is to be found the spiritual
ancestry of a religion that reads Christianity exclusively
in terms of salvation and will have nothing to do with
'fiat creation' or the divine justice or heaven or hell or
the living and holy God." And so for the cry of the
older Liberalism: "Back to Christ"—upon which Dr.
McGiffert has put, we trust, a final quietus—there is
now apparently to be substituted the cry: "Back to
the non-theistic Gentile Christians who read Christianity only in terms of salvation and were not interested in theology or in God." But if that really is to
be the cry, the outlook is very dark. It is a sad thing
if the continuity of Christianity can be saved only by

[6] *Op. cit.*, p. 87.

an appeal to the non-theistic Gentile Christians. For
those non-theistic Gentile Christians never really existed
at all.

The truth is that the antitheistic or non-theistic religion of the present day—popularized by many
preachers and undergirded by scholars such as the author
of the brilliant book of which we have just been speaking—the truth is that this non-theistic religion, which,
at least in one of its most characteristic forms, takes the
man Jesus of naturalistic reconstruction as its only God,
will have to stand at last upon its own feet. With the
historic Christian Church, at any rate, it plainly has
little to do. For the Christian Church can never relinquish belief in the heavenly Father whom Jesus
taught His disciples to love.

At the root, then, of faith in God, as taught in the
Bible, is simply theism: the belief, namely, that the
universe was created and is now upheld by a personal
Being upon whom it is dependent but who is not dependent upon it. God is, indeed, according to this
Christian view, immanent in the world, but He is also
personally distinct from the world, and from the finite
creatures that He has made. The transcendence of God
—what the Bible calls the "holiness" of God—is at the
foundation of Christian faith. The Christian trusts
God because God has been pleased to reveal Himself
as one whom it is reasonable to trust; faith in God is
based on knowledge.

Certainly that knowledge does not remove our feeling of wonder in the presence of God, but should rather
deepen it till it leads to a boundless awe. Some things

have been revealed to us about God, and they are by far the greatest things that have ever entered the mind of man; but how limited they are compared to the boundless mystery of the unknown! If a man's knowledge of God removes his sense of wonder in the presence of the Infinite One, he shows thereby that he has hardly begun to have any true knowledge at all.

Yet partial knowledge is not necessarily false; and the partial knowledge that we have of God, though it leaves vast mysteries unexplored, is yet sufficient as a basis for faith. If such a God be for us, the Christian can say, who can be against us? Such a God is One whom a man can trust.

At this point it may be well to pause for a few moments at the text from the eighth chapter of Romans, which we have just quoted. "If God be for us," says Paul, "who can be against us?"[7]

These words constitute a veritable battle cry of faith; they might have served as the motto for countless heroic deeds. Trusting in the God of Israel, men fought mighty battles and won glorious victories; the Lord of hosts is a powerful ally.

Jonathan thought so, when he and his armourbearer made that foolhardy attempt upon a garrison of the Philistines. "There is no restraint to the Lord," he said, "to save by many or by few." David thought so, with his five smooth stones from the brook and his great boasting adversary. "Thou comest to me," he said, "with a sword, and with a spear, and with a shield: but I come to thee in the name of the Lord of

---

[7] Rom. viii: 31.

hosts, the God of the armies of Israel." Elisha thought
so, when he and his servant were shut up in Dothan.
The Syrians had sought to take his life; he had revealed
their plans to the king of Israel; and at last they had
caught him fair. When the servant of the prophet
arose in the morning, the city was all surrounded by the
Syrian hosts. "Alas, my master," he said, "how shall
we do?" But the prophet was not dismayed. "Open
his eyes," he said, "that he may see." And the Lord
opened his eyes, and behold the hills were covered not
only by the Syrian armies, but also by the fiery horses
and chariots of God's protecting care. The apostles
thought that God was a powerful ally, when they testified in the council of the Jews: "We must obey God
rather than men." Luther thought so on that memor-
able day when he stood before kings and princes, and
said—in substance even if not in word—"Here I stand,
I cannot do otherwise, God help me! Amen."

In these great moments of history the hand of God
was revealed. But, alas, the thing is not always so
plain. Many prophets as true as Elisha have been surrounded by the armies of the aliens, and no fiery horses
and chariots have put in an appearance; five smooth
stones from the brook, even when slung bravely in the
name of the Lord of hosts, are not always able to cope
with modern artillery; many men of God as bold as
Peter, as sturdy as good Luther, have testified faithfully
to the truth, and, being unprotected by the favor of the
people or by wise Gamaliels or by friendly Electors of
Saxony, have gone to the stake for their pains. Nor
does it always seem to be true that the blood of the

martyrs is the seed of the Church. Persecution sometimes seems to be crowned with a tragic success. As
when pure religion by the use of physical weapons was
largely stamped out of Italy and Spain and France, so
often the blood of the martyrs seems to be shed in vain.
What is true, moreover, in the large arena of history
is also true in our workaday lives. Sometimes, in times
of great spiritual crisis, the hand of God is revealed;
there has been a signal answer to prayer; deliverance
has come in wondrous ways when expected least. But
at other times prayer just as earnest seems to go un-
answered, and faith seems set at naught.

In our perplexity we are sometimes tempted to think
of our God very much as He was thought of on one
occasion by the enemies of Israel. "Their gods," they
said with reference to Israel, "are gods of the hills . . . .
but let us fight against them in the plain, and surely we
shall be stronger than they:"[8] So our God, we are sometimes tempted to say, can help us in some of the circum-
stances of life; but at other times, whether by the lack
of the power or by the lack of the will—it makes little
practical difference—at other times He fails. Religion.
we say, will help sometimes; but there are troubles in
which some far more definite assistance is required; our
God is a God of the hills, but beware, O Christian, of
the plain.

Such doubts, in the text to which we have referred,
are all brushed grandly aside. "If God be for us," says
Paul, "who can be against us?" The challenge, in the
Apostle's mind, can receive no answer; if God be for

---

[8] I Kings, xx: 23.

us, none can be against us—none in hill or dale, in
cloud or sunshine, in life or death, among things present
or things to come.

Such a faith is magnificent; it is heroic; it fires the
imagination and stirs the will. What a glorious thing
it is, to be sure, when a strong man stands with God
against the world! But mere magnificence is not
enough, and a lurking doubt remains. The belief of
Paul is magnificent, but is it founded upon sober truth?
Is God, as we know Him, really sufficient not merely
for some, but for all, of our needs?

The answer to that question obviously depends upon
what you think of God. If God be merely the tribal
divinity of a people of the hills, as He was thought to
be by those enemies mentioned in the twentieth chapter
of the First Book of Kings, then certainly we cannot
expect Him to fight for us in the plain. Of course the
polytheism of those Syrians is gone for good; it may
almost evoke a smile. But other errors, though more
refined, are equally fatal to the comfort of Paul's words.
There are ways of thinking about God, widely prevalent today, which make Him of even less value than a
local divinity of the Israelitish hills.

Some of these ways of thinking have already been
mentioned. There is, for example, the common view
which identifies God with the totality of the world.
That view goes by different names, and most commonly
by no name at all. It may best be called pantheism.
But we ought not to be confused by a technical term;
whatever may be thought of the name, the thing itself
is not confined to the philosophers. It is sometimes

called the "new theology;" it is sometimes called (quite
falsely) the doctrine of divine "immanence."   But it
is, at any rate, a mistake to think that it affects only
the classroom; on the contrary, it affects the plain man
as well as the scholar, and not only the pulpit but the
pew.   In the religious life of our day it is almost dominant; few of us can altogether escape its influence.
Certainly it is nothing new; far from being the "new
revelation" which it is sometimes represented as being,
it is really as old as the hills; for millenniums it has
been in the world dulling the moral sense and blighting
the religious life of man.   But it has never been more
powerful than it is today.

We find ourselves in this world in the midst of a
mighty process.   It manifests itself in the wonders of
the starry heavens, and in the equal wonders that the
microscope has revealed.   It is seen in the revolving
seasons, and in the achievements of the human mind.
In the presence of it, we stand in awe; we are impressed
by our own littleness; we are but infinitesimal parts of
a mighty whole.   And to that whole, to that mighty,
all-embracing world-process, which we moderns have
learned with a new clearness to regard as one, the pantheist applies the dread name of God.   God is thus no
longer thought of as an artificer apart from his machine;
He is thought of as naught but the universe itself, conceived of not in its individual manifestations, but as a
mighty whole.

Who does not appreciate the appeal of such a view?
It has stimulated some of the profoundest thinking and
inspired some of the grandest poetry of the race.

But it contains no comfort whatever for oppressed and burdened souls. If God be but another name for the totality of things, then when we possess Him we possess nothing that we did not have before. There is then no appeal from the world to Him; when the world treats us ill, there is no help for us, for we have already had our "God." "If God be for us, who can be against us?"—these words were spoken by no pantheist, but by one who could appeal from nature to nature's God.

That appeal is possible only if God is a free and holy Person, eternally sovereign over all that He has made. True, He is immanent in the world; He is no far-off deity separate from His works. There is an important truth in pantheism; the Christian too can say, "In Him we live, and move, and have our being," and "Closer is He than breathing, and nearer than hands and feet." God is present in the world; not a single thing that happens is independent of Him. But that does not mean that He is identical with the world or limited by it; because the world is dependent upon Him, it does not follow that He is dependent upon the world. He is present in the world not because He is identical with it, but because He is Master of it; the universe is pervaded and enveloped by the mystery of His will. These things have been hidden from the wise and prudent and revealed unto babes. It is simplicity that is here profound; the stupendous wonder of God's works, the boundless complexity of His universe, should never be allowed to conceal the simple fact that He is a Person; that simple fact, the child's possession of every

trusting soul, is the greatest mystery of all. Jesus
taught, indeed, the immanence of God; He saw God's
hand in the sprouting of the seed; not a sparrow, He
said, could fall to the ground without God.   That
might have been said by the philosophers.   But Jesus
did not put it merely in that form; what He said was,
"One of them shall not fall on the ground *without your
Father."*   And when He said that, the long searchings
of philosophy were over, and He whom men had dimly
felt for, the personal, living God, was revealed.

If, then, there is to be an appeal from nature to nature's God, if there is to be real faith, God must be
thought of as a God who can work wonders; not as
another name for the totality of existing things, but as
a free and living Person.   Think of Him otherwise,
and you remain forever bound in the prison-house of
the world.

But another form of error is equally fatal.   It is a
homelier, less pretentious form of error, but it is equally
destructive of a faith like the faith of Paul.   We have
insisted that God is free, that He can govern the course
of nature in accordance with His will; and it is an important truth indeed.   But many men make of it the
only truth, and in doing so they make shipwreck of
their faith.   They think of God *only* as one who can
direct the course of nature for their benefit; they value
Him only for the things that He can give.

We are subject to many pressing needs, and we are
too much inclined to value God, not for His own sake,
but only because He can satisfy those needs.   There is
the need of food and clothing, for ourselves and for our

loved ones, and we value God because He can answer the petition, "Give us this day our daily bread." There is the need of companionship; we shrink from loneliness; we would be surrounded by those who love us and those whom we can love. And we value God as one who can satisfy that need by giving us family and friends. There is the need of inspiring labor; we would be delivered from an aimless life; we desire opportunities for noble and unselfish service of our fellowmen. And we value God as one who by His ordering of our lives can set before us an open door.

These are lofty desires. But there is one desire that is loftier still. It is the desire for God Himself. That desire, too often, we forget. We value God solely for the things that He can do; we make of Him a mere means to an ulterior end. And God refuses to be treated so; such a religion always fails in the hour of need. If we have regarded religion merely as a means of getting things—even lofty and unselfish things—then when the things that have been gotten are destroyed, our faith will fail. When loved ones are taken away, when disappointment comes and failure, when noble ambitions are set at naught, then we turn away from God; we have tried religion, we say, we have tried prayer, and it has failed. Of course it has failed! God is not content to be an instrument in our hand or a servant at our beck and call. He is not content to minister to the worldly needs of those who care not a bit for Him. The text in the eighth chapter of Romans does not mean that religion provides a certain formula for obtaining worldly benefits—even the high-

est and most ennobling and most unselfish of worldly
benefits. "If God be for us, who can be against us?"—
that does not mean that faith in God will bring us
everything that we desire. What it does mean is that
if we possess God, then we can meet with equanimity
the loss of all besides. Has it never dawned upon us
that God is valuable for His own sake, that just as personal communion is the highest thing that we know
on earth, so personal communion with God is the sub-
limest height of all? If we value God for His own
sake, then the loss of other things will draw us all the
closer to Him; we shall then have recourse to Him in
time of trouble as to the shadow of a great rock in a
weary land. I do not mean that the Christian need
expect always to be poor and sick and lonely and to
seek his comfort only in a mystic experience with His
God. This universe is God's world; its blessings are
showered upon His creatures even now; and in His own
good time, when the period of its groaning and travail-
ing is over, He will fashion it as a habitation of glory.
But what I do mean is that if here and now we have
the one inestimable gift of God's presence and favor,
then all the rest can wait till God's good time.

If, then, communion with God is the one great possession, worth more than all the rest besides, how shall
we attain unto it—how shall we come to know God?

Many men, as has already been observed, are telling
us that we should not seek to *know* Him at all; theology, we are told, is the death of religion. We do not
know God, then—such seems to be the logical implication of this view—but simply feel Him. In its con-

sistent form such a view is mysticism; religion is reduced to a state of the soul in which the mind and the
will are in abeyance. Whatever may be thought of such
a religion, I cannot see that it possesses any moral quality at all; pure feeling is non-moral, and so is religion
that is not founded upon theology. What makes our
love for a true friend, for example, such an ennobling
thing is the recognition by our mind of the character
of our friend. Human affection, so beautiful in its
apparent simplicity, really depends upon a treasured host
of observations of the actions of our friend. So it is
also in the case of our relation to God. It is because
we know certain things about Him, it is because we
know that He is mighty and holy and loving, that our
communion with Him obtains its peculiar quality. The
devout man cannot be indifferent to doctrine, in the
sense in which many modern preachers would have us
be indifferent, any more than he can listen with equanimity to misrepresentations of an earthly friend. Our
faith in God, despite all that is said, is indissolubly connected with what we *think* of Him. The devout man
may indeed well do without a complete systematization
of his knowledge—though if he be really devout he
will desire just as complete a systematization as he can
possibly obtain—but some knowledge he certainly must
have.

How then may we attain to this knowledge of God
that is so necessary to faith; how may we become acquainted with Him? We may do so, I think, in the
old, old ways; I have no entirely new ways to suggest.

First of all, we may do so by a contemplation of His

works in nature. "The invisible things of him from the creation of the world are clearly seen, being understood by the things that are made, even his eternal power and Godhead." "The heavens declare the glory of God; and the firmament showeth his handywork." By some men, indeed, the glory is unperceived. There are some men who look upon a mountain as a mere mass of rock and stone, a thunderstorm as a mere phenomenon of the atmosphere, and a fair flower as a mere combination of leaves and petals. God pity them—the poor blind souls! But when the eyes of our souls are opened, then as we stand before a great mountain range we shall say: "I will lift up mine eyes unto the hills: from whence shall my help come?"; in the fury of the storm we shall think of Him who did fly upon the wings of the wind; and the flowers of the field will reveal to us the weaving of God—and even Solomon in all his glory was not arrayed like one of these.

In the second place, God is known by His voice within us. The contemplation of the universe, of which we have just spoken, brings us to the very brink of infinity; the world is too vast for us, and all around it is enveloped by an impenetrable mystery. But there is also an infinity within. It is revealed in the voice of conscience. In the sense of guilt there is something that is removed from all relativity; we stand there face to face with the absolute. True, in the humdrum of life we often forget; but the strange experience comes ever again. It may be in the reading or witnessing of a great drama; the great tragedies, in the world's literature, are those that pull aside the curtain of the com-

monplace and makes us feel anew the stark irrevocableness of guilt. It may also be, alas, in the contemplation of our own lives. But however conscience speaks,
it is the voice of God. The law reveals a Lawgiver;
and the character of this law reveals the Lawgiver's
awful righteousness.

In the third place, God is known through the Bible.
And He is known through the Bible in an entirely fresh
and peculiar way. True, the Bible does repeat and en-
force what ought to have been learned elsewhere; it
does reinforce the voices of nature and of conscience; it
tells us anew that the heavens declare the glory of God;
it presents the law of conscience with a new and terrible
earnestness as the law of God. But it does far more
than all that; it also presents God in loving action, in
the course of history, for the salvation of sinful men.
From Genesis to Revelation, from Eden to Calvary, as
the covenant God of Israel and as the God and Father
of our Lord Jesus Christ, all through the varied course
of Bible story, God appears in the fulfilment of one loving plan. The marvel is that it is so plainly the same
God throughout. The manner of His action varies;
we see various aspects of His person; He appears in anger
as well as in love. But it is plainly the same Person
throughout: we rise from the Bible—I think we can
say it without irreverence—with a knowledge of the
character of God. There is a real analogy here to our
relation with an earthly friend. How do we come to
know one another? Not all at once, but by years of
observation of one another's actions. We have seen a
friend in time of danger, and he has been brave; we

have gone to him in perplexity, and he has been wise; we have had recourse to him in time of trouble, and he has given us his sympathy. So gradually, with the years, on the basis of many, many such experiences, we have come to love him and revere him. And now just a look or a word or a tone of his voice will bring the whole personality before us like a flash; the varied experiences of the years have been merged by some strange chemistry of the soul into a unity of affection. So it is, somewhat, with the knowledge of God that we obtain from the Bible. In the Bible we see God in action; we see Him in fiery indignation wiping out the foulness of Sodom; we see Him leading Israel like a flock; we see Him giving His only begotten Son for the sins of the world. And by what we see we learn to know Him. In all His varied dealings with His people He has never failed; so now we know Him and adore Him. Such knowledge seems to be a simple, an instinctive, thing; the varied dealings of God with His people have come together in the unity of our adoration. And now He is revealed as by a flash by every smallest dispensation of His providence, whether it be in joy or whether it be in sorrow.

As thus made known, surely God is sufficient for all our needs. There is no limit to His power; if He be our champion, we need not fear what principalities and powers and the whole universe can do. He alone is righteous; His presence will make us spotless as the light. He is loving, and His love will cast out fear. Truly we can say with Paul: "If such a God be for us, who can be against us?"

But that text begins with "if," and it is a stupendous "if." "*If* God be for us"—but is God for us? Many persons, it is true, trip along very lightly over that "if"; they have no doubt about the matter; they are quite sure that God is for them. But the curious thing is that those who have no doubt about the matter are often just the ones who are most sadly wrong. The people of Jerusalem at the time of Jeremiah had no doubt; they were quite sure that God was for them; but they went into exile all the same; God was not for them at all. The Jews in the days of John the Baptist had no doubt; were they not God's chosen people? Even in the darkest days of Roman rule they were quite sure that God would give them the victory. But as a matter of fact the axe was even then laid at the root of the tree. The Pharisee in the parable was quite sure that God was for him when he went up into the Temple to pray—"God, I thank thee that I am not as other men are . . . . or even as this publican." But the publican, it will be remembered, went down into his house justified rather than he.

These men were all quite sure that God was for them, but they were all entirely wrong. How then may we be sure; and if we become sure, is not our assurance a delusion and a snare? How can we remove the "if" of this text: how can we be sure that God *is* for us?

There are only two possible ways.

One way is to do what is right. God always stands for the right; if we are right, then no matter what men and demons may do God is on our side. But are we

right? The Pharisee was quite sure that he was right,
but as a matter of fact he was most terribly wrong.
May we not be equally mistaken?

No doubt we think we can avoid the Pharisee's
error. God was not for him, we say, because he was
sinfully contemptuous toward that publican; we will
be tender to the publican, as Jesus has taught us to be,
and then God will be for us. It is no doubt a good
idea; it is well that we are tender toward the publican.
But what is our attitude toward the Pharisee? Alas,
we despise him in a truly Pharisaical manner. We go
up into the temple to pray; we stand and pray thus
with ourselves: "God I thank thee that I am not as
other men are, proud of my own righteousness, un-
charitable toward publicans, or even as this—Pharisee."
Can we really venture thus, as the Pharisee did, to stand
upon our obedience of God's law, as being better than
that of other men, whether publicans or Pharisees, in
order to assure ourselves of God's favor?

Paul at least said, "No!"; and surely Paul has some
right to be heard, since it is he who gave us the heroic
text to which we have turned. Paul had tried that
method, and it had failed; and the seventh chapter of
Romans is a mighty monument of its failure. The
power of the flesh is too strong; we are living over an
abyss of sin and guilt. Of course we may forget what
lies beneath; we may forget if we are willing to live
on the surface of life and be morally blind like the
Jews before the exile or the Pharisee who went up into
the Temple to pray. But when the eyes of our souls
are opened, when we catch a terrifying glimpse of the

righteousness of God, then we are in despair. We try to escape; we try to balance the good in our lives against the evil; we give tithes of all we possess; we point frantically to our efforts as social workers; and thus we try to forget the terrible guilt of the heart. Such is the bondage of the law.

But why should we not give up the struggle? It is so hopeless, and at the same time so unnecessary. Is God for us, despite our sin? Joyfully the Christian answers, "Yes." But why is He for us? Simple indeed is the Christian answer to that question: He is for us simply because He has chosen to be. He surely has a right to receive whom He will into His fellowship: and as a matter of fact He has chosen to receive us poor sinners who trust in Christ; He chose to receive us when He gave Christ to die. It was His act, not ours. The "if" of the text is a stupendous "if"; but such a word is not allowed to stand very long in the eighth chapter of Romans. "If God be for us, who can be against us?"—it is a large "if," but it melts away very soon in the warmth of God's grace. "If God be for us, who can be against us? He that spared not his own Son, but delivered him up for us all, how shall he not with him also freely give us all things? Who shall lay anything to the charge of God's elect? It is God that justifieth. Who is he that condemneth?"

Appeal to God's act alone can enable us to face every adversary. It can of course enable us to face the unjust condemnation of men. What care we what men may say, if we have the approval of God? But it can do vastly more than that; it can enable us to face not only the unjust condemnation of men, but the condemnation of men that is perfectly just. And nothing else on earth or in heaven can enable us to do that. There are some things that the world never forgives; Peter could never, I suppose, have been received again into the society of gentlemen after he had played the traitor under fire. But God chose to receive him, and upon the rock of his faith the Church was built. There may be some foul spot in our lives; the kind of thing that the world never forgives, the kind of thing, at any rate, for which we who know all can never forgive ourselves. But what care we whether the world forgives, or even whether we can forgive ourselves, if God forgives, if God has received us by the death of His Son? That is what Paul means by "boasting" in the Cross of Christ. If we could appeal to God's approval as ours by right, how bravely we should boast—boast in the presence of a world of enemies! If God knows that we are right, what care we for the blame of men? Such boasting, indeed, can never be ours. But we can boast in what God has done. Little care we whether our sin be thought unpardonable or no, little interested are we in the exact calculation of our guilt. Heap it up mountain high, yet God has removed it all. We cannot explain God's act; it is done on His responsibility, not ours. "I know not," the Christian says, "what my guilt may be; one thing I know: Christ loved me and gave Himself for me. Come on now ye moralists of the world, come on ye hosts of demons, with your whisperings of hell! We fear you not; we take our stand beneath the shadow of the Cross, and standing there, in God's favor, we are safe. No fear of challenge now! If God be for us, who can be against us? None, in heaven or in earth or in hell. 'Neither death, nor life, nor angels, nor principalities, nor powers, nor things present, nor things to come, nor height, nor depth, nor any other creature, shall be able to separate us from the love of God, which is in Christ Jesus our Lord.' "

CHAPTER III

FAITH IN CHRIST

It appears from what has just been said that although theism is necessary to the Christian's faith in God, it is not all that is necessary. It is impossible to trust God in the Christian sense without holding that He is a free and living Person, Creator and Ruler of the world; but it is also impossible to trust Him without convictions that go far beyond that. Indeed the Christian doctrine of God in itself, far from leading to faith, would lead only to despair; for the clearer be our view of God's righteousness, the deeper becomes our consciousness of guilt. God has done all things well; we are His creatures upon whom He has showered His bounty; but a mighty barrier has been placed between us and Him by the fact of sin.

That fact is recognized in the Bible from beginning to end; and it is recognized with particular clearness in the teaching of Jesus. Jesus does indeed speak much of the Fatherhood of God, and His words are full of comfort for those who are God's children. But never does He speak of God as being the Father of all men; in the Sermon on the Mount those who can say, "Our Father which art in heaven," are distinguished in the sharpest possible way from the world outside. Our Lord came not to teach men that they were already sons of God, but to make them sons of God by His redeeming work.   The Fatherhood of God as it is taught in the New Testament designates not a relationship in which God stands to all men, but a relationship in which He stands to those who have been redeemed.

That assertion may be surprising to men who have never turned from what is said about the New Testament to what the New Testament says itself; but it is unquestionably true.   It needs, however, to be guarded against two misunderstandings.

In the first place, it does not mean that the New Testament ignores those features in the relationship of God to all men which are analogous to the relationship in which an earthly father stands to his children.   God is the Author of the being of all men, whether Christians or not; He cares for all; He showers His bounty upon all: and apparently the New Testament does here and there even use the term Father to designate this broader relationship.   But what we are insisting upon is that such a use of the term is to say the least highly exceptional, and that it does not enter into the heart of what the New Testament means by the Fatherhood of God.   It is not that the doctrine of the universal fatherly relationship in which God stands to His creatures is unimportant; indeed a large part of our previous discussion has been taken up with showing how very important it is; but our point is that the New Testament ordinarily reserves the tender words, "Father" and "Son," to describe a far more intimate relationship.   Everything in the Bible is concerned with the fact of sin; the relationship in which man as man stood to God has been broken by transgression, and only when that barrier is removed is there sonship worthy of the name. Thus we are not saying that the doctrine of the universal Fatherhood of God is untrue: but what we are saying is that far from being the essence of Christianity, it is only the presupposition of Christianity; it is only the starting-point which the New Testament finds in "natural religion" for the proclamation of the gospel of divine grace.

The second misunderstanding which needs to be guarded against is the common impression that there is something narrow about what we have designated as the New Testament doctrine of the Fatherhood of God. How narrow a thing it is, the modern man exclaims, to hold that God is the Father of some and not of all! This objection ignores the central thing in the New Testament teaching, and the central thing in Christianity; it ignores the Cross of Christ. It is true that men are separated from God by the awful fact of sin; it is true that sonship worthy of the name is possessed only by those who are within the household of faith: but what men do not seem to understand is that the door of the household of faith is open wide for all men to come in. Christ died to open that door, and the pity is that we try to close it by our failure to spread the invitation throughout all the world. As Christians we ought certainly to love all our fellow-men everywhere, including those who have not yet come to Christ; but if we really love them, we shall show our love not by trying to make them content with a cold natural religion, but by bringing them in, through the proclamation of the gospel, into the warmth and joy of the household of faith.

In the Bible, then, it is not merely God as Creator who is the object of faith, but also, and primarily, God as Redeemer from sin. We fear God because of our guilt; but we trust Him because of His grace. We trust Him because He has brought us by the Cross of Christ, despite all our sin, into His holy presence. Faith in God depends altogether upon His redeeming work.

That fact explains an important feature of the New Testament teaching about faith—the feature, namely, that the New Testament ordinarily designates as the object of faith not God the Father but the Lord Jesus Christ. The New Testament does indeed speak of faith in God, but it speaks more frequently of faith in Christ.

The importance of this observation must indeed not be exaggerated; no man can have faith in Christ without also having faith in God the Father and in the Holy Spirit. All three persons of the blessed Trinity are according to the New Testament active in redemption; and all three therefore may be the object of faith when redemption is accepted by sinful men.

Redemption was accomplished, however, according to the New Testament, by an event in the external world, at a definite time in the world's history, when the Lord Jesus died upon the cross and rose again. In Christ the redeeming work of God became visible; it is Christ, therefore, very naturally, who is ordinarily represented as the object of faith.

But as in the case of God the Father, so in the case

of Christ, it is impossible to have faith in a person without having knowledge of the person; faith is always based upon knowledge.

That important principle is denied by many persons in the modern world in the case of Christ, just as we have seen that it is denied in the case of God the Father.

It was denied in typical fashion, for example, in a sermon which I remember hearing some years ago. The subject of the sermon was the incident of the healing of the centurion's servant.[1] That centurion, the distinguished preacher said in effect, knew nothing about theology; he knew nothing about the Nicene or Chalcedonian doctrine of the Person of Christ; he knew nothing about the creeds: but he simply trusted Jesus, and Jesus praised his faith in the highest terms. So we also, it was said in effect, may be quite indifferent to the theological controversy now raging in the Church, and like the centurion may simply take Jesus at His word and do what Jesus says.

From the point of view of common-sense reading of the Bible that sermon was surely quite incorrect; it was rather an extreme instance of that anti-historical forcing of the plain words of the Bible which is so marked a feature of the intellectual decadence of the present day. Where is it said in the Gospel narrative that the centurion obyed Jesus' commands; where is it said that he *did* anything at all? The point of the narrative is not that he did anything, but rather that he did nothing; he simply believed that Jesus could do something, and accepted that thing at Jesus' hands; he simply be-

---
[1] Luke vii: 2-10; Matt. viii: 5-13.

lieved that Jesus could work the stupendous miracle of healing at a distance. In other words, the centurion is presented as one who had faith; and faith, as distinguished from the effects of faith, consists not in doing something but in receiving something. Faith may result in action, and certainly true faith in Jesus always will result in action; but faith itself is not doing but receiving.

But the sermon in question was not merely faulty from the point of view of common-sense reading of the Bible; it was also faulty from the point of view of psychology. The centurion, it was said in effect, knew nothing about the Christology of the creeds; he knew nothing about the doctrine of the two natures in the one person of our Lord; yet he believed in Jesus all the same. Clearly the inference intended to be drawn was that opinions about Jesus are matter of indifference to faith in Jesus; no matter what a man thinks about the person of Christ, it was maintained in effect, he may still trust Christ.

That principle is maintained with the greatest confidence by present-day writers and speakers on the subject of religion. But surely it is quite absurd. Let us see how it would work out in ordinary life. Can it really be held that I can trust a person irrespective of the opinions that I hold about the person? A simple example may make the matter clear.

Suppose I have a sum of money to invest. It may be rather a wild supposition—but just let us suppose. I have a sum of money to invest, and not knowing much about the stock market I go to an acquaintance

of mine and ask him to invest my savings for me.   But
another acquaintance of mine hears of it and injects a
word of caution.

"You are certainly taking a great risk," he says to
me.   "What do you know about the man to whom
you are entrusting your hard-earned savings?   Are you
sure that he is the kind of man that you ought to trust?"

In reply I say that I do know certain things about
the man.   "Some time ago he came to this town and
succeeded in selling the unwary inhabitants of it some
utterly worthless oil-stock; and if he is not in jail, he
certainly ought to be there.   But," I continue, "opinions about a person may differ—that is merely an intellectual matter—and yet one may have faith in the person; faith is quite distinct from knowledge.   Consequently I can avoid the unpleasant duty of raking up
the past of the speculative gentleman in question; I can
avoid unseemly controversy as to whether he is a rascal
or not, and can simply trust him all the same."

Of course if I talked in that way about so serious a
thing as dollars and cents, I should probably be regarded
as needing a guardian; and I might soon find my property being better managed for me than I could manage
it for myself: yet it is just exactly in that way that
men talk with regard to the subject of religion; it is
just in that way that they talk with regard to Jesus.
But is it not quite absurd?   Surely it is impossible to
trust a person whom one holds in one's mind to be
untrustworthy.   Yet if so, we cannot possibly be indifferent to what is called the "theological" controversy
of the present day; for that controversy concerns just

exactly the question whether Jesus is trustworthy or not. By one party in the Church Jesus is presented as One in whom men can have confidence in this world and the world to come; by the other party He is so presented as that trust in Him would be ignoble if not absurd.

Yet there may be an objection. "Faith," it may be said, "seems to be such a wonderfully simple thing. What has the simple trust which that centurion reposed in Jesus to do with the subtleties of the Chalcedonian creed? What has it to do even with a question of fact like the question of the virgin birth? And may we not return from our theology, or from our discussion of details of the New Testament presentation, to the simplicity of the centurion's faith?"

To this objection there is of course one very easy answer. The plain fact is that we are by no means in the same situation as the centurion was with reference to Jesus; we of the twentieth century need to know very much more about Jesus in order to trust Him than the centurion needed to know. If we had Jesus with us in bodily presence now, it is quite possible that we might be able to trust Him with very little knowledge indeed; the majesty of His bearing might conceivably inspire unbounded confidence almost at first sight. But as a matter of fact we are separated from Him by nineteen centuries; and if we are to commit ourselves unreservedly to a Jew who lived nineteen hundred years ago, as to a living person, there are obviously many things about Him that we need to know. For one thing, we need to know that He is alive; we need to know, there-

fore, about the resurrection. And then we need to
know how it is that He can touch our lives; and that
involves a knowledge of the atonement and of the way
in which He saves us from our sin. But it is useless
to enter into further detail. Obviously it is a very
strange thing that persons of the twentieth century
should come into a relation of living trust with a man
of the first century; and if they are to do so, they must
know much more about Him than His contemporaries
needed to know. Even if the centurion, therefore,
could get along with very little knowledge of the person
of Christ, it does not follow that we can do so.

There is, however, another answer to the objection.
Men say that faith—for example the faith of the centurion—is a simple thing and has nothing to do with
theology. But is faith really so simple a thing? The
answer is not so obvious as many persons suppose.
Many things which seem to be simple are really highly
complex. And such is the case with respect to trust in
a person. Why is it that I trust one man and do not
trust another? Sometimes it may seem to be a simple
thing; sometimes I trust a man at first sight; trust in
these cases seems to be instinctive. But surely "instinct" in human beings is not so simple as it seems.
It really depends upon a host of observations about the
personal bearing of men who are trustworthy and those
who are not trustworthy. And usually trust is not
even apparently instinctive; usually it is built up by
long years of observation of the person who is trusted.
Why do I trust this man or that? Surely it is because
I know him; I have seen him tried again and again, and

he has rung true. The result seems to be very simple; at the end a look or a tone of the voice is sufficient to give me as in a flash an impression of the whole person. But that impression is really the result of many things that I know. And I can never be indifferent to what is said about the one whom I trust; I am indignant about slanders directed against him, and I seek to defend my high opinion of him by an appeal to the facts.

So it is in the case of our relation to Jesus. We are committing to Him the most precious thing that we possess—our own immortal souls, and the destinies of society. It is a stupendous act of trust. And it can be justified only by an appeal to facts.

But what becomes, then, it may be asked, of the childlike faith which seems to be commended by our Lord Himself? If faith is so elaborate an intellectual affair, how could Jesus ever have said: "Whosoever shall not receive the kingdom of God as a little child, he shall not enter therein."[2] Surely a little child does not wait until all probabilities have been weighed, and until the trustworthiness of its parents has been established at the bar of reason, before it reaches out its little hands in simple trust.

In answer, three things need to be said.

In the first place, in holding that knowledge is logically the basis of faith we are not holding that it necessarily precedes faith in the order of time. Sometimes faith in a person and knowledge of the person come in the same instant. Certainly we are not maintaining that faith in Jesus has to wait until a man has learned

[2] Mark, x: 15.

all that the theologians or even all that the Bible can tell him about Jesus; on the contrary, faith may come first, on the basis of very elementary knowledge, and then fuller knowledge may come later.   Indeed that is no doubt quite the normal order of Christian experience.   But what we do maintain is that at no point is faith independent of the knowledge upon which it is logically based; even at the very beginning faith contains an intellectual element; and if the subsequent increase of knowledge should show the person in whom trust is reposed to be untrustworthy, the faith would be destroyed.

In the second place, the question may well be asked whether the faith of a child, after all, is independent of knowledge.   We for our part think that it is not, provided the child has come to the age of conscious personal life.   The child possesses, stored up in its memory, experiences of the mother's goodness, knows how to distinguish her from other persons, and hence smiles at her approach.   Very different is the non-theological "faith" of the modern pragmatist, that can subsist independently of the opinions which may be held as to the object of faith.   Whatever may be said for that pragmatist attitude, it is certainly as unchildlike as anything that could possibly be imagined.   A child never trusts a person whom it holds with its mind to be untrustworthy.   The faith of the modern pragmatist is a very subtle, sophisticated, unchildlike thing; what is really childlike is the faith that is founded upon knowledge of the one in whom trust is reposed.

There is, indeed, perhaps one stage of childhood

where the intellect is in abeyance; but it is the stage where conscious personal life has not yet been begun. Is it that stage to which Christian faith ought to return? There are many who answer this question, implicitly if not explicitly, in the affirmative; these are the mystics, who hold that religion is an ineffable experience in which the ordinary faculties of the soul are quiescent, and who must hold, if they be consistent, that the goal of religion is a sheer loss of individual consciousness through the merging of the soul in the abyss of the divine. It is toward such mysticism that the modern depreciation of the intellect in religion really tends. No doubt the anti-intellectualism of our day does not often consciously go so far; but that is not because the starting-point is right, but because the way has not yet been followed to the end. The ultimate goal of the modern view of faith is a nirvana in which personality is lost.

In the third place, we have so far really not gotten at what Jesus meant at all. When our Lord bade His disciples receive the kingdom of heaven as little children, was it really the ignorance of the little children to which He appealed? We think not. No, it was not the ignorance of children to which our Lord appealed, but their conscious helplessness, their willingness to receive a gift. What mars the simplicity of the childlike faith which Jesus commends is not an admixture of knowledge, but an admixture of self-trust. To receive the kingdom as a little child is to receive it as a free gift without seeking in slightest measure to earn it for one's self. There is a rebuke here for any attempt to earn

salvation by one's character, by one's own obedience to
God's commands, by one's own establishment in one's
life of "the principles of Jesus"; but there is no rebuke
whatever for an intelligent faith that is founded upon
the facts.   The childlike simplicity of faith is marred
sometimes by ignorance, but never by knowledge; it
will never be marred—and never has been marred in the
lives of the great theologians—by the blessed knowledge of God and of the Saviour Jesus Christ which is
contained in the Word of God.   Without that knowledge we might be tempted to trust partly in ourselves;
but with it we trust wholly to God.   The more we
know of God, the more unreservedly we trust Him;
the greater be our progress in theology, the simpler and
more childlike will be our faith.

There is no reason, then, for us to modify the conclusion to which we were led by an examination of
the centurion's faith; faith in Christ, we hold, can be
justified only by an appeal to facts.

The facts which justify our appeal to Jesus concern
not only His goodness but also His power.   We might
be convinced of His goodness, and yet not trust Him
with these eternal concerns of the soul.   He might
have the will to help and not the power.   We might
be in the position of the ship-captain's child in the
touching story, who, when all on shipboard were in
terror because of an awful storm, learned that his father
was on the bridge and went peacefully to sleep.   The
confidence of the child very probably was misplaced;
but it was misplaced not because the captain was not
faithful and good, but because the best of men has no

power to command the wind and the sea that they should obey him. Is our confidence in Jesus equally misplaced? It is misplaced if Jesus was the poor, weak enthusiast that He is represented as being by naturalistic historians. But very different is the case if He was the mighty Person presented in the Word of God. The question as to which was the real Jesus may be decided in one way or it may be decided in the other; but at any rate it cannot be ignored. We cannot trust Jesus if Jesus is unworthy of our trust.

Why then do those who reduce Jesus to the level of humanity, who regard Him (if traditional language be stripped off) simply as a Jewish teacher of long ago, the initiator of the "Christ-life"—why do such persons speak of having "faith in Jesus"? They do so, I think, because they are slipping insensibly into a wrong use of terms; when they say "faith in Jesus," they mean really not faith in Jesus but merely faith in the teaching and example of Jesus. And that is a very different thing. It is one thing to hold that the ethical principles which Jesus enunciated will solve the problems of society, and quite another thing to come into that intimate, present relation to Him which we call faith; it is one thing to follow the example of Jesus and quite a different thing to trust Him. A man can admire General Washington, for example, and accept the principles of his life; yet one cannot be said to trust him, for the simple reason that he died over a hundred years ago. His soldiers could trust him; for in their day he was alive; but we cannot trust him, because now he is dead. And when persons who believe that

Jesus was simply a great teacher of long ago, and are not particularly interested in any personal identity between that mystic experience which they call "Christ" in the soul and the historic person Jesus of Nazareth— when such persons speak of "faith in Jesus," the expression is merely a survival, now meaningless, of a usage which had meaning only when Jesus was regarded as what He is said in the New Testament to be.   Real faith in Jesus can exist only when the lofty claims of Jesus are taken as sober fact, and when He is regarded as the eternal Son of God, come voluntarily to earth for our redemption, manifesting His glory even in the days of His flesh, and now risen from the dead and holding communion with those who commit their lives to Him.

The truth is that in great sections of the modern Church Jesus is no longer the object of faith, but has become merely an example for faith; religion is based no longer upon faith in Jesus but upon a faith in God that is, or is conceived to be, like the faith that Jesus had in God.

This mighty transition is often unconscious; by a loose use of traditional language men have concealed from themselves as well as from others the decisive step that has really been taken.   By no means all, it is true, of those who have taken the step have been thus self-deceived; there are among them some real students of history who detect clearly the momentous difference between a faith in Jesus and a faith in God that is like Jesus' faith.   For such scholars the origin of "faith in Jesus" becomes the most important problem in the entire history of religion. How was it that a Jewish teacher, who (in accordance with modern naturalism) did not exceed the limits of humanity, came to be taken as the object of religious faith; how and when did men add to a faith in God that was like Jesus' faith a faith in Jesus Himself? However and whenever this event took place, it was certainly a momentous event. Of course to anyone who accepts the testimony of the Bible the problem is quickly solved; the New Testament throughout—the Gospels as well as the Epistles—depicts Jesus of Nazareth as one who from the beginning presented Himself, and with full justification, as the object of faith to sinful men. But to modern naturalistic historians the problem remains; and by the more thoughtful of them it is placed in the very forefront of interest. How was there added to faith in God, encouraged and inspired by Jesus, a faith in Jesus Himself?

Many solutions of this problem have been proposed in the course of modern criticism, but none of them has won universal acceptance. According to the older Liberalism, represented, for example, by Harnack, faith in Jesus as Redeemer, in the Pauline sense, was merely the temporary form in which the religious experience brought about by contact with the real Jesus had to be expressed in the forms of thought proper to that day. According to a radical like Bousset, on the other hand, faith in Jesus arose in Damascus or Antioch, when, in a meeting of the disciples full of ecstatic phenomena, someone uttered the momentous words,

"Jesus is Lord," and thus the One who in Jerusalem had been regarded as absent in heaven came to be regarded as present in the Church and hence as being the object of faith.   Many other solutions, or varieties of the few generically differing solutions, have been proposed.   But it cannot be said that any one of them has been successful. Modern naturalism so far has expended all its learning and all its ingenuity in vain upon the question how it was that a Jew of the first century came to be taken as the object of religious faith, despite the strictness of Jewish monotheism, by contemporaries belonging to His own race.

Yet although we do not think that scholars like Bousset have been successful in solving the problem, they have at least seen clearly what the problem is; and that is great gain. They have seen clearly that faith in Christ is quite different from a faith merely like Christ's faith; and they have seen clearly that not the latter but the former is characteristic of the historic Christian Church.   If the choice of the Church is now to be reversed, the radicalness of the decision should not be ignored.

Such clearness, however, is, unfortunately, in many quarters conspicuous by its absence; there are many who by a sort of spiritual indolence or at least timorousness seek to conceal the issue both from themselves and from others.   It is evident that they have a sentimental attachment to Jesus; it is evident that they love Him; why then should they try to decide whether such attachment is or is not what is designated by the New Testament and by the historic Church as "faith"?

"Surely," men say, "it is better to let sleeping dogs lie; surely it is better not to mar the peace of the Church by too careful an effort at definition of terms. If those who are called 'Liberals' in the Church will only consent to employ traditional language, if they will only avoid offending friend as well as foe by the unpardonable ecclesiastical sin of plainness of speech, all will be well, and the work of the Church can go satisfactorily on as though there were no division of opinion at all."

Many are the ways in which such a policy is commended to our favor; plausible indeed are the methods by which Satan seeks to commend an untruth; often the Tempter speaks through the lips of sincere and good men. "Let us alone," some devout pastors say, "we are preaching the gospel; we are bringing men and women into the Church; we have no time for doctrinal controversy; let us above all have peace." Or else it is the greatness and beneficence of the work of the organized Church which catches the imagination and inspires the cry of "peace and work." "Let us sink our doctrinal differences," it is urged, "and go on with our work; let us quit defending Christianity and proceed to propagate it; whatever be our theological differences let us conquer the world for Christ."

Plausible words these are, and uttered sometimes no doubt, by truly Christian men. For such men we have full sympathy: their eyes are closed; they have no inkling of the facts; they have no notion how serious is the issue that faces the Church. But for us, and for all who are aware of what is really going on, the policy of

"peace and work," the policy of concealment and pallia-
tion, would be the deadliest of sins.   The Church is
placed before a serious choice; it must decide whether it
will merely try to trust God as Jesus trusted Him, or
whether it will continue to put its trust in Jesus Himself.   Upon that choice depends the question which of
two mutually exclusive religions is to be maintained.
One of the two is the redemptive religion known as
Christianity; the other is a religion of optimistic confidence in human nature, which at almost every conceivable point is the reverse of Christian belief.   We must
decide which of the two we shall choose.   But above
all things let us choose with our eyes open; and when
we have chosen let us put our whole souls into the
propagation of what we believe.   If Christ is the object
of faith, as He is held by the New Testament to be, then
let us proclaim Him not only in our pulpits but by all
our activity in the Church.   There is nothing more unreasonable than to preach the gospel with our lips and
then combat the gospel through the funds that we contribute to agencies and boards or through the votes that
we cast in Church councils and courts.

It is the encouragement of such inconsistency that
places the most serious ethical stain upon Modernism
in evangelical churches today.   It is not a stain which
appears merely in weaknesses and inconsistencies of individual men—for such failings we have the greatest
possible sympathy, being keenly conscious of worse
moral failures in ourselves than can be found in other
men—but it is a stain that is inherent in the settled
policy of a great party in the Church.   Concealment of

the issue, the attempt to slur over a mighty change as though full continuity were being preserved, the double use of traditional language, the acceptance on false pretences of the support of old-fashioned evangelical men and women who have no inkling of what is really being done with their contributions or with their votes—these are things that would convince us, even prior to historical or theological investigation, that there is something radically wrong with the Modernist movement of the present day.   "By their fruits ye shall know them," said our Lord,[3] and judged by that ethical standard the present movement will not stand the test. There are, indeed, exceptions to the particular fault upon which we are now insisting—for example the exception formed by the honesty of the Unitarian Churches, for which we have the very highest possible respect—but the chief outward successes of Modernism have been won by the wrong methods of which we speak.   A true Reformation would be characterized by just what is missing in the Modernism of the present day; it would be characterized above all by an heroic honesty which for the sake of principle would push all consideration of consequences aside.

Such a Reformation we on our part believe to be needed today; only, we believe that it would be brought about, not by a new religion which consists in imitation of the reduced Jesus of modern naturalism, but by the rediscovery of the gospel of Christ.   This is not the first time in the history of the world when the gospel has been obscured.   It was obscured in the Middle Ages,

---

[3] Matt. vii: 20.

for example; and how long and how dark, in some respects, was that time! But the gospel burst forth with new power—the same gospel that Paul and Augustine had proclaimed. So it may be in our own day; the gospel may come forth again to bring light and liberty to mankind. But this new Reformation for which we long will not be brought about by human persuasions, or by consideration of consequences, or by those who seek to save souls through a skillful use of ecclesiastical influences, or by those who refrain from speaking the truth through a fear of "splitting the Church" or of making a poor showing in columns of Church statistics. How petty, in the great day when the Spirit of God again moves in the Church, all such considerations will seem! No, when the true Reformation comes, it will come through the instrumentality of those upon whom God has laid His hand, to whom the gospel has become a burning fire within them, who speak because they are compelled to speak, who, caring nothing for human influences and conciliation and external Church combinations and the praise or blame of men, speak the word that God has given them and trust for the results to Him alone. In other words, it will be brought about by men of faith.

We do not know when such an event will come; and when it comes it will not be the work of men but the work of the Spirit of God. But its coming will be prepared for, at any rate, not by the concealment of issues, but by clear presentation of them; not by peace in the Church between Christian and anti-Christian forces, but by earnest discussion; not by darkness, but

by the light. Certainly it will not be hindered by an
earnest endeavor to understand what faith in Christ
really is, and how it differs from a faith that is merely
an attempt at imitating Christ's faith.

Such an endeavor may perhaps be furthered by a consideration of one or two of the shibboleths which appear
in the religious literature of the day. Nothing like completeness will be necessary; we may begin at almost any
point in the literature of the Modernist movement, in
order to discover the root from which it all comes.

There is, for example, the alternative between a gospel *about* Jesus, and the gospel *of* Jesus. The Church,
it is said, has been so much concerned with a gospel
about Jesus that the gospel of Jesus has been neglected;
we ought to reverse the process and proclaim the gospel
that Jesus Himself proclaimed.

With regard to this proposal, it should be noticed
that even in its relation to the question of the seat of
authority in religion, it is not so innocent as it might
seem. It proposes that the seat of authority shall be
"the teachings of Christ." But the seat of authority
for the historic Church has been not merely the teachings of Christ, but the whole Bible. For the Bible,
therefore, which was formerly regarded as the Word of
God, is to be substituted the very small part of the Bible
which consists in the words which Jesus spoke when
He was on earth. Certainly there are difficulties connected with such a change, due, for example, to the
fact that Jesus, who is to be held as the supreme and sole
authority, placed at the very basis of His own life and
teaching that view of the authority of the whole Bible

which is here so lightly being abandoned. The view
which regards the "teachings of Christ" as the sole
authority seems therefore to be self-contradictory; for
the authority of Christ establishes the authority of the
Bible.   The truth is that "the teachings of Christ" can
be truly honored only when they are taken as an organic
part of the divine revelation found in the Scriptures
from Genesis to Revelation; to isolate Christ from the
Bible is to dishonor Christ and reject His teaching.

But the point now is not that the substitution of
the teachings of Jesus for the whole Bible as the seat
of authority in religion is unjustifiable, but rather that
it is at any rate momentous.   If it must be accomplished, let it at least be accomplished with full understanding of the importance of the step.

The true seriousness of the substitution of the gospel
of Jesus for a gospel about Jesus is not, however, limited
to the bearing of this step upon the question of the seat
of authority in religion; even more serious is the different attitude toward Jesus which the step involves.   The
advocates of a "gospel of Jesus" in the modern sense
seem to imagine that the acceptance of such a gospel
brings Jesus closer to us than is done by the acceptance
of a gospel about Jesus.   In reality, the exact opposite
is the case.   Of course if the "gospel about Jesus" is
not true, if it sets forth not the facts that inhere in
Jesus Himself, but merely the false opinions of other
persons about Him, or "interpretations" of Him which
have merely temporary validity, then the gospel about
Jesus does place a veil of falsehood between Jesus and
us and should be rejected in order that we may find

contact with Him as He actually was. But entirely different is the case if the gospel about Jesus sets forth the facts. In that case that gospel brings us into a kind of contact with Him compared with which the mere acceptance of a gospel which He Himself proclaimed is a very cold and distant thing.

Acceptance of what Jesus Himself proclaimed does not in itself mean any more than that He is taken as a teacher and leader; it is only what might conceivably be done in the case of many other men. A man can, for example, accept the gospel of Paul; that means merely that he holds the teaching of Paul to be true: but he cannot accept a gospel about Paul; for that would give to the apostle a prerogative that belongs only to his Lord. Paul himself expressed what we mean when he wrote to the Corinthians: "Was Paul crucified for you"?[4] The great apostle to the Gentiles, in other words, proclaimed a gospel; but he was not himself the substance of the gospel, the latter prerogative being reserved for Jesus Himself. A gospel *about* Jesus exalts Jesus, therefore, and brings Him into far closer contact with us than could ever be done by a gospel *of* Jesus.

But what was this gospel which Jesus proclaimed, this gospel that is now to replace the gospel about Him which has been proclaimed by the Apostle Paul and by the historic Church? Our only knowledge of it is obtained from the words of Jesus that are recorded in the New Testament. But those words as they stand make it abundantly plain that the gospel which Jesus proclaimed was also, at its very centre, a gospel about Him;

---

[4] I Cor. i: 13.

it did far more than set forth a way of approach to God which Jesus Himself followed, for it presented Jesus as Himself the way which could be followed by sinful men. According to the New Testament our Lord even in the days of His flesh presented Himself not merely as Teacher and Example and Leader but also, and primarily, as Saviour; He offered Himself to sinful men as One who alone could give them entrance into the Kingdom of God; everything in His teaching pointed forward to His redeeming work in His death and resurrection; the culmination of Jesus' gospel was the Cross. The significance of redemption could not, indeed, be fully pointed out until redemption had actually been accomplished; and our Lord therefore pointed forward to the fuller revelation which was to be given through His apostles: but, although only by way of prophecy, yet clearly enough, He did, even when He was on earth, tell men what He had come into the world to do. "The Son of Man," He said, "came not to be ministered unto, but to minister, and to give His life a ransom for many."[5]

So much will perhaps be generally admitted: if the words of Jesus as they are recorded in the Gospels are accepted as authentic, then the separation of the gospel about Jesus from a gospel of Jesus is radically false; for the gospel about Jesus (which is the gospel that all through the centuries has brought peace to burdened souls) was also the gospel which Jesus Himself, even in the days of His flesh, proclaimed.

If, then, we are to obtain a Jesus who kept His own

[5] Mark x: 45.

Person out of His gospel, and offered to men merely the way of approach to God which He had followed for Himself, we cannot do so by an acceptance of the New Testament account of Jesus' words as it stands, but can do so, if at all, only by a critical process within that account.   The true words of Jesus must be separated from words falsely attributed to Him before we can obtain the modern gospel which omits redemption and the Cross.

But that critical process, upon investigation, is found to be impossible.   Even in the earliest sources supposed, rightly or wrongly, by modern criticism to underly our Gospels, Jesus presented Himself not merely as an example for faith but as the object of faith.[6]   He invited men not merely to have faith in God like the faith which He had in God, but He invited them to have faith in Him.   He clearly regarded Himself as Messiah, not in some lower meaning of the word, but as the heavenly Son of Man who was to come with the clouds of heaven and be the instrument in judging the world; He clearly pointed forward to some catastrophic event in which He was to have a central place, some catastrophic event by which the Kingdom of Heaven was to be ushered in. The truth is that the Jesus who preached a gospel of universal divine fatherhood and a sonship which was man's right as man never existed until modern times; the real Jesus presented Himself not merely as Teacher but also as Lord and as Redeemer.   If, therefore, we are to hold to the real "gospel of Jesus," we must also

[6] See James Denney, *Jesus and the Gospel*, 1909.

hold to "the gospel about Jesus," and the separation between the two must be given up.

Another way in which the opposition between a religion that makes Jesus merely the example for faith and a religion that makes Him primarily the object of faith appears in the modern world, is to be found in the varying answers to the question whether Jesus was or was not a "Christian." According to a very widespread way of thinking Jesus was the Founder of the Christian religion because He was the first to live the Christian life, in other words because He was Himself the first Christian. According to our view, on the other hand, Jesus stands in a far more fundamental and intimate relation to Christianity than that; He was, we hold, the Founder of our religion not because He was the first Christian, but because He made Christianity possible by His redeeming work.

At no point does the issue in the modern religious world appear in more characteristic fashion than just here. Many persons hold up their hands in amazement at our assertion that Jesus was not a Christian, while we in turn regard it as the very height of blasphemy to say that He was a Christian. "Christianity," to us, is a way of getting rid of sin; and therefore to say that Jesus was a Christian would be to deny His holiness.

"But," it is said, "do you mean to tell us that if a man lives a life like the life of Jesus but rejects the doctrine of the redeeming work of Christ in His death and resurrection, he is not a Christian?" The question, in one form or another, is often asked; but the answer is very simple. Of course if a man really lives a life

like the life of Jesus, all is well; such a man is indeed
not a Christian, but he is something better than a Christian—he is a being who has never lost his high estate of
sonship with God.   But our trouble is that our lives,
to say nothing of the lives of these who so confidently
appeal to their own similarity to Jesus, do not seem to
be like the life of Jesus.   Unlike Jesus, we are sinners,
and hence, unlike Him, we become Christians; we are
sinners, and hence we accept with thankfulness the redeeming love of the Lord Jesus Christ, who had pity on
us and made us right with God, through no merit of
our own, by His atoning death.

That certainly does not mean that the example of
Jesus is not important to the Christian; on the contrary,
it is the daily guide of his life, without which he would
be like a ship without a rudder on an uncharted sea.
But the example of Jesus is useful to the Christian not
prior to redemption, but subsequent to it.

In one sense indeed it is useful prior to redemption:
it is useful in order to bring a sinful man into despair
of ever pleasing God by his own efforts; for if the life
of Jesus be the life that God requires, who can stand in
His holy presence?   Thus to the unredeemed the example of Jesus has an important part in the proclamation of that terrible law of God which is the schoolmaster to bring men unto Christ; it serves by its lofty
purity to produce the consciousness of sin and thus to
lead men to the Cross.

But so far as any comfort or positive help is concerned, the example of Christ is useful only to those
who have already been redeemed.   We disagree very

strongly therefore with those teachers and preachers who think that Jesus should first be presented as a leader and example in order that afterwards, perhaps, He may be presented as Saviour; we deprecate the popular books for young people which appeal to the sense of loyalty as the first way of approach to Jesus; it seems to us very patronizing and indeed blasphemous when, for example, Jesus' choice of a life-work is presented as a guide toward the choice of a life-work on the part of boys and young men. The whole method, we think, is wrong. The example of Jesus is, indeed, important, but it is not primary; the first impression to give to a child is not that of the ways in which Jesus is like us but that of the ways in which He differs from us; He should be presented first as Saviour and only afterwards as Example; appeal should be made not to latent forces capable of following Jesus' example but to the sense of sin and need.

Let it not be said that this method of approach is ill suited to the young, and founded on a false psychology; on the contrary, its effectiveness has been proved through the long centuries of the Church's life. Now that it has largely been abandoned boys and girls drift away from the Church, whereas when it was followed they grew up into stalwart Christian men and women. It is very natural for a child of the covenant to learn first to trust Christ as Saviour almost as soon as conscious life begins, and then, having become God's child through Him, to follow His blessed example. There is a child's hymn—a child's hymn that I think the Christian can never outgrow—which puts the matter right:

> O dearly, dearly has He loved,
> And we must love Him too,
> And trust in His redeeming blood,
> And try His works to do.

That is the true order of Christian pedagogy—"trust in His redeeming blood" first, and then "try His works to do." Disaster will always follow when that order is reversed.

The Lord Jesus, then, came into this world not primarily to say something, not even to be something, but to do something; He came not merely to lead men through His example out into a "larger life," but to give life, through His death and resurrection, to those who were dead in trespasses and sins; we are Christians not because we have faith in God like the faith in God which Jesus Himself had, but because we have faith in Him.

But can we really have faith in Him? We cannot do so if He be the mere initiator of the "Christ life" who is presented in much modern preaching; but we can do so if He be the living Saviour presented in the Word of God.

One fearful doubt, however, still assails us. It comes from what may be called the cosmic aspects of human life, from the dread thought of the infinite abyss which is all about us as we walk upon this earth.

Reflections on the nothingness of human life, it must be admitted, are often rather dull; they clothe themselves readily in cant. But if a thing is true, it cannot become false by being hackneyed. And as a matter of fact, it cannot be denied that man is imprisoned on one of the smaller of the planets, that he is enveloped by infinity on all sides, and that He lives but for a day in what seems to be a pitiless procession. The things in which he is interested, the whole of his world, form but an imperceptible oasis in the desert of immensity. Strange it is that he can be absorbed in things which from the vantage ground of infinity must seem smaller than the smallest playthings.

It cannot be denied: man is a finite creature; he is a denizen of the earth. From one point of view he is very much like the beasts that perish; like them he lives in a world of phenomena; he is subject to a succession of experiences, and he does not understand any one of them. Science can observe; it cannot explain: if it tries to explain, it ceases to be science and sometimes becomes almost laughable. Man is certainly finite.

But that is not the whole truth. Man is not only finite; for he knows that he is finite, and that knowledge brings him into connection with infinity. He lives in a finite world, but he knows, at least, that it is not the totality of things. He lives in a procession of phenomena, but to save his life he cannot help searching for a first cause. In the midst of his trivial life, there rises in his mind one strange and overpowering thought—the thought of God. It may come by reflection, by subtle argument from effect to cause, from the design to the designer. Or it may come by a "sunset touch." Back of the red, mysterious, terrible, silent depths, beyond the silent meeting place of

sea and sky, there is an inscrutable power.   In the presence of it man is helpless as a stick or stone.   He is as
helpless, but more unhappy—unhappy because of fear.
With what assurance can we meet the infinite power?
Its works in nature, despite all nature's beauty, are horrible in the infliction of suffering.   And what if physical suffering should not be all; what of the sense of
guilt; what if the condemnation of conscience should
be but the foretaste of judgment; what if contact with
the infinite should be contact with a dreadful infinity
of holiness; what if the inscrutable cause of all things
should turn out to be, after all, a righteous God?

This great beyond of mystery—can Jesus help us
there?   Make Him as great as you will, and still He
may seem to be insufficient.   Extend the domains of
His power far beyond our ken, and still there may seem
to be a shelving brink with the infinite beyond.   And
still we are subject to fear.   The mysterious power that
explains the world still, we say, will sweep in and
overwhelm us and our Saviour alike.   We are of all
men most miserable; we had trusted in Christ; He carried us a little on our way, and then left us, helpless
as before, on the brink of eternity.   There is for us no
hope; we stand defenseless at length in the presence of
unfathomed mystery, unless— a wild, fantastic thought
—unless our Saviour, this Jesus in whom we had
trusted, were Himself in mysterious union with the
eternal God.   Then comes the full, rich consolation
of God's Word—the mysterious sentence in Philippians:
"who, being in the form of God, thought it not robbery
to be equal with God"; the strange cosmology of Col-

ossians: "who is the image of the invisible God, the first-born of every creature: for by him were all things created, that are in heaven, and that are in earth, visible and invisible, whether they be thrones, or dominions, or principalities, or powers: all things were created by him, and for him: and he is before all things, and by him all things consist"; the majestic prologue of the Fourth Gospel: "In the beginning was the Word, and the Word was with God, and the Word was God"; the mysterious consciousness of Jesus: "All things are delivered unto me of my Father: and no man knoweth the Son, but the Father; neither knoweth any man the Father, save the Son, and he to whomsoever the Son will reveal him."

These things have been despised as idle speculation, but in reality they are the very breath of our Christian lives.   They are, indeed, the battle ground of theologians; the Church hurled anathemas at those who held that Christ, though great, was less than God.   But those anathemas were beneficent and right.   That difference of opinion was no trifle; there is no such thing as "almost God."   The thought is blasphemy; the next thing less than the infinite is infinitely less.   If Christ be the greatest of finite creatures, then still our hearts are restless, still we are mere seekers after God.   But now is Christ, our Saviour, the One who says, "Thy sins are forgiven thee," revealed as very God.   And we believe.   It is the supreme venture of faith; faith can go no higher.   Such a faith is a mystery to us who possess it; it is ridiculed by those who have it not.   But if possessed it overcomes the world.   In Christ all things

are ours.   There is now for us no awful Beyond of
mystery and fear.   We cannot, indeed, explain the
world, but we rejoice now that we cannot explain it;
to us it is all unknown, but it contains no mysteries for
our Saviour; He is on the throne; He is at the centre;
He is ground and explanation of all things; He pervades
the remotest bounds; by Him all things consist.   The
world is full of dread, mysterious powers; they touch
us already in a thousand woes.   But from all of them
we are safe.   "Who shall separate us from the love of
Christ?   Shall tribulation, or distress, or persecution,
or famine, or nakedness, or peril, or sword?   As it is
written, For thy sake we are killed all the day long; we
are accounted as sheep for the slaughter.   Nay, in all
these things we are more than conquerors through Him
that loved us.   For I am persuaded, that neither death,
nor life, nor angels, nor principalities, nor powers, nor
things present, nor things to come, nor height, nor
depth, nor any other creature, shall be able to separate
us from the love of God, which is in Christ Jesus our
Lord."

CHAPTER IV

FAITH BORN OF NEED

It has been shown in the last chapter that the Jesus who is presented in the New Testament is one whom a man can trust; there are no limits to His goodness and no limits to His power. But that presentation in itself does not afford a sufficient basis for faith; no matter how great and good be the Saviour, we cannot trust Him unless there be some contact specifically between ourselves and Him. Faith in a person involves not merely the conviction that the person trusted is able to save, but also the conviction that he is able and willing to save *us;* that there should be faith, there must be some definite relation between the person trusted and a specific need of the person who trusts. The men and women to whom Jesus said in the Gospels (in substance or in word): "Thy faith hath saved thee; go in peace," all had very definite needs that they trusted Jesus to relieve. One was sick, one was deaf, one was blind; and when they came to Jesus they were not merely convinced that He was in general a powerful healer, but each of them was convinced, more or less firmly, that He could heal his peculiar infirmity, and each of them sought healing in his own specific case. So it is with us today. It is not enough for us to know that Jesus is great and good; it is not enough for us to know that He was instrumental in the creation of the world and that He is now seated on the throne of all being.   These things are indeed necessary to faith, but they are not all that is necessary; if we are to trust Jesus, we must come to Him personally and individually with some need of the soul which He alone can relieve.

That need of the soul from which Jesus alone can save is sin.   But when I say "sin," I do not mean merely the sins of the world or the sins of other people, but I mean your sin—your sin and mine.   Consideration of the sins of other people is the deadliest of moral anodynes; it relieves the pain of conscience, but it also destroys moral life.   Very different is that conviction of sin which leads a man to have faith in Christ.

That true conviction of sin appears as the prerequisite of faith in a great verse in the Epistle to the Galatians, which describes in briefest compass the true Christian way of approach to Christ.   "Wherefore," says Paul, "the law was our schoolmaster to bring us unto Christ."[1]   No doubt Paul is referring specifically to the law of Moses as the schoolmaster to bring the Jews to Christ; but we are fully justified in giving the verse a far wider application.   The particular way in which the Old Testament law, according to Paul, led the Jews to Christ was that it brought them to despair because of their sin, and so made them willing to accept the Saviour when He came.   The "schoolmaster" of the Pauline figure of speech was not, in ancient life, a teacher; but he was a slave appointed in well-to-do families of the time to go with the children to school and in general prevent them from having any liberty.   The

[1] Gal. iii: 24.

figure of speech in that verse is only slightly varied, therefore, from that which appears just before, where the law is represented as a jailer.   But for the law, Paul means, the Jews might have thought that their own righteousness was sufficient; but every time that they were tempted to seek escape from condemnation, the high standard of the law showed to them how very far short they had come of the will of God, and so they were prevented from false hopes.

Of course, this is only one aspect of the old dispensation; even under the old dispensation, according to Paul, there was faith as well as law; the grace of God was revealed as well as His awful righteousness; the religion of the Old Testament is by no means represented by Paul as one of unrelieved gloom.   But so far as man's own efforts were concerned, the gloom, according to Paul, was complete; hope was to be found, not in man, but in God's gracious promise of a salvation that was to come.

Thus the law of Moses, according to Paul, was a schoolmaster to bring the Jews to Christ because it produced the consciousness of sin.   But if so, it is natural to suppose that any revelation of the law of God which, like the law of Moses, produces the consciousness of sin may similarly serve as a schoolmaster unto Christ.   Indeed we have direct warrant for this wide extension of the application of the verse.   "When the Gentiles," Paul says in another passage, "which have not the law, do by nature the things contained in the law, these, having not the law, are a law unto themselves."[2]   Here

---

[2] Rom. ii: 14.

the law of Moses is plainly brought into relation to a
law under which all men stand; the Old Testament
Scriptures make the law of God plainer than it is to
other men, but all men have received, in their con-
sciences, some manifestation of God's will, and are without excuse when they disobey. However the law is
manifested, then, whether in the Old Testament, or
(still more clearly) in the teaching and example of
Jesus, or in the voice of conscience, it may be a schoolmaster to bring men to Christ if it produces the consciousness of sin.

That is the old way of coming to Christ—first peni-
tence at the dread voice of the law, then joy at the gracious invitation of the Saviour. But that way, in recent years, is being sadly neglected; nothing is more characteristic of present religious conditions than the loss of
the consciousness of sin; confidence in human resources
has now been substituted for the thankful acceptance
of the grace of God.

This confidence in human resources is expressed in
many ways; it is expressed even in prayer. I remember
a service which I attended a year or so ago in an attrac-
tive village church. The preacher, who was a well-edu-
cated, earnest man, had at least the courage of his convictions, and gave expression to his optimistic religion
of humanity not only in his sermon but also in his
prayers. After quoting the verse in Jeremiah which
reads, "The heart is deceitful above all things, and desperately wicked,"[3] he said, in effect (though I cannot
remember his exact words): "O Lord, thou knowest

---

[3] Jer. xvii: 9.

that we cannot accept this interpretation; for we believe that man does not will to do evil but fails only from lack of knowledge." That was at least frank and consistent, and I must confess that I had much more respect for it than for the pious phrases in which the modern religion of humanity is usually veiled. It was paganism pure and simple, but it was at least a respectable paganism not afraid of plainness of speech. And indeed it ought not to be forgotten that paganism can be a very respectable thing; the modern confidence in man is not unlike that of the ancient Stoics; and Stoicism, with its doctrine of a universal human brotherhood and its anticipations of modern humanitarian effort, has some high ethical achievements to its account.

But the gospel of paganism, ancient and modern, the gospel that a preacher, whom I heard preach recently, commended as "the simple gospel of human worth," has its limitations; its optimism remains, after all, upon the surface of life, and underneath there are depths that it can never touch. It is at any rate quite different from Christian belief; for at the root of Christianity is a profound consciousness of sin. Superficially, indeed, there is some similarity; the Modernist preacher speaks with apparent humility of the sad defects of human life, and of the need of divine assistance. But such humility does not touch the heart of the matter at all; indeed it really implies a similarity in kind, though not in degree, between what now is and what ought to be. Very different is the Christian attitude. To the Christian, sin does not differ from goodness merely in the degree which achievement has attained; but it is regarded as transgression of a law that is absolutely fixed; the pagan sense of imperfection is widely different from the Christian sense of sin.

At the root of the Christian attitude is a profound consciousness of the majesty of the moral law. But the majesty of the moral law is obscured in many ways at the present time, and most seriously of all in the sphere of education. Indeed, strangely enough, it is obscured in the sphere of education just by those who are becoming most keenly conscious of the moral bankruptcy of modern life. There is something radically wrong with our public education, it is said; an education that trains the mind without training the moral sense is a menace to civilization rather than a help; and something must quickly be done to check the impending moral collapse. To meet this need, various provisions are being made for moral training in our American public schools; various ethical codes are being formed for the instruction of children who are under the care of the State. But the sad thing is that these efforts are only making the situation tenfold worse; far from checking the ravages of immorality, they are for the most part themselves non-moral at the root. Sometimes they are also faulty in details, as when a recent moral code indulges in a veiled anti-Christian polemic by a reference to differences of "creed" that will no doubt be taken as belittling, and adopts the pagan notion of a human brotherhood already established, in distinction from the Christian notion of a brotherhood to be established by bringing men into a common union with Christ. But the real objection to some, if not all, of these efforts

does not depend upon details; it depends rather upon
the fact that the basis of the effort is radically wrong.
The radical error appears with particular clearness in
a "Children's Morality Code" recently proposed by
"The Character Education Institution" in Washington.
That code contains eleven divisions, the sub-headings
of which are as follows: I, "Good Americans Control
Themselves"; II, "Good Americans Try to Gain and
Keep Good Health"; III, "Good Americans are Kind";
IV, "Good Americans Play Fair"; V, "Good Amer-
icans are Self-Reliant"; VI, "Good Americans Do Their
Duty"; VII, "Good Americans are Reliable"; VIII,
"Good Americans are True"; IX, "Good Americans
Try to do the Right Thing in the Right Way"; X,
"Good Americans Work in Friendly Cooperation with
Fellow-Workers"; XI, "Good Americans are Loyal."

Here we have morality regarded as a consequence of
patriotism; the experience of the nation is regarded as
the norm by which a morality code is to be formulated.
This (thoroughly non-moral) principle appears in
particularly crass form in "Point Two" of the Institution's *Five-Point Plan for Character Education in
Elementary School Classrooms*: "The teacher," says the
pamphlet, "presents the Children's Morality Code as a
reliable statement of the conduct which is considered
right among boys and girls who are loyal to Uncle
Sam, and which is justified by the experience of multitudes of worthy citizens who have been Uncle Sam's
boys and girls since the foundation of the nation.   The
teacher advises the children to study this Morality Code

in order to find out what Uncle Sam thinks is
right. . . ."

But what of those not infrequent cases where what
"Uncle Sam" thinks is right is what God thinks is
wrong?   To say to a child, "Do not tell a lie because
you are an American," is at bottom an immoral thing.
The right thing to say is, "Do not tell a lie because it
is wrong to tell a lie."   And I do not think that it is
an unconstitutional intrusion of religion into the public schools for a teacher to say that.

In general, the holier-than-thou attitude toward other
peoples, which seems to be implied in the program of
the Character Education Institution almost from beginning to end, is surely, at the present crisis in the history
of the world, nothing short of appalling.   The child
ought indeed to be taught to love America, and to feel
that whether it is good or bad it is *our* country.   But
the love of country is a very tender thing, and the
best way to kill it is to attempt to inculcate it by
force.   And to teach, in defiance of the facts, that
honesty and kindness and purity are peculiarly American virtues—this is surely harmful in the extreme.
We blamed Germany, rightly or wrongly, for this kind
of thing; yet now in the name of patriotism we advocate as truculent an inculcation of the same spirit as
Prussia could ever have been accused of at its worst.
Surely the only truly patriotic thing to teach the child
is that there is one majestic moral law to which our own
country and all the countries of the world are subject.

But the most serious fault of this program for "character building" is that it makes morality a product of

experience, that it finds the norm of right conduct in
the determination of that "which is justified by the
experience of multitudes of worthy citizens who have
been Uncle Sam's boys and girls since the foundation of the nation." That is wrong, as we have already observed, because it bases morality upon the experience of the nation; but it would also be wrong if it
based it upon the experience of the whole human race.
A code which is the mere result of human experimenta-
tion is not morality at all (despite the lowly etymolog-
ical origin of our English word), but it is the negation
of morality. And certainly it will not work. Moral
standards were powerful only when they were invested
with an unearthly glory and were treated as quite different in kind from all rules of expediency. The truth
is that decency cannot be produced without principle.
It is useless to try to keep back the raging sea of passion
with the flimsy mud-embankments of an appeal to experience. Instead, there will have to be recourse again,
despite the props afforded by the materialistic paternal-
ism of the modern State, to the stern, solid masonry of
the law of God. An authority which is man-made can
never secure the reverence of man; society can endure
only if it is founded upon the rock of God's commands.

It will not now be possible to propose in full our
own solution of the difficult educational problem of
which we have just been speaking. We have indeed
such a solution. Most important of all, we think, is
the encouragement of private schools and Church
schools; a secularized public education, though perhaps
necessary, is a necessary evil; the true hope of any

people lies in a kind of education in which learning and piety go hand and hand. Christianity, we believe, is founded upon a body of facts; it is, therefore, a thing that must be taught; and it should be taught in Christian schools.

But taking the public school as an established institution, and as being, under present conditions, necessary, there are certain ways in which the danger of that institution may be diminished.

1. The function of the public school should be limited rather than increased. The present tendency to usurp parental authority should be checked.

2. The public school should pay attention to the limited, but highly important, function which it is now neglecting—namely, the impartation of knowledge.

3. The moral influence of the public-school teacher should be exerted in practical rather than in theoretical ways. Certainly the (thoroughly destructive and immoral) grounding of morality in experience should be avoided. Unfortunately, the true grounding of morality in the will of God may, in our public schools, also have to be avoided. But if the teacher himself knows the absolute distinction between right and wrong, his personal influence, without theoretical grounding and without "morality codes," will appeal to the distinction between right and wrong which is implanted in the soul of the child, and the moral tone of the school will be maintained. We do not for a moment mean that that sort of training is sufficient; for the only true grounding of morality is found in the revealed will of God: but at least it will avoid doing harm.

4.   The public-school system should be kept healthy by the absolutely free possibility of the competition of private schools and Church schools, and the State should refrain from such regulation of these schools as to make their freedom illusory.

5.   Uniformity in education—the tendency which is manifested in the proposal of a Federal department of education in the United States—should be avoided as one of the very greatest calamities into which any nation can fall.

6.   The reading of selected passages from the Bible, in which Jews and Catholics and Protestants and others can presumably agree, should not be encouraged, and still less should be required by law.   The real centre of the Bible is redemption; and to create the impression that other things in the Bible contain any hope for humanity apart from that is to contradict the Bible at its root.   Even the best of books, if it is presented in garbled form, may be made to say the exact opposite of what it means.

7.   Public-school children should be released at certain convenient hours during the week, so that the parents, if they choose, may provide for their religious instruction; but the State should entirely refrain both from granting school credit for work done in these hours and from exercising any control whatever either upon attendance or upon the character of the instruction.

Such are in general the alternative proposals that we might make if we were dealing with the problem which has led to the efforts at "character building" of which we have spoken. We recognize to the full the good motives of those who are making such efforts; but the efforts are vitiated by the false principle that morality is based upon experience; and so they will only serve, yet further, we fear, to undermine in the hearts of the people a sense of the majesty of the law of God.

Certainly if there be no absolute law of God, there can be no consciousness of sin; and if there be no consciousness of sin, there can be no faith in the Saviour Jesus Christ. It is no wonder that many persons regard Jesus merely as the initiator of a "Christ life" into which they are perfectly able, without more ado, to enter; it is no wonder that they regard their lives as differing only in degree from His. They will never catch a real glimpse of the majesty of His Person and they will never understand His redeeming work, until they come again into contact with the majesty of the law. Then and then only will they recognize their sin and need, and so come to that renunciation of all confidence in themselves which is the basis of faith.

It must be admitted that this way of approach to Christ is often rough and thorny. That does not mean, indeed, that faith in Christ must always be preceded by agony of soul. Almost unlimited is the variety of Christian experience; and often faith seems to come at the same moment as contrition. The children of Christian parents, in particular, often come to trust Christ as their Saviour almost as soon as consciousness begins; these children of the covenant know the grace of God almost as soon as they know sin. But whatever be the particular form of Christian experience, the way of approach to Christ through the law of God always involves a rebuke to human pride.

It is not surprising, therefore, that other ways of approach are often proposed. This way being rough and thorny, other ways are being sought. It seems hard to many men to enter into the Christian life through the little wicket gate; and many therefore are clambering up over the wall.

In the first place, there is the purely intellectual way. The claims of Christianity, it is said, must be investigated on their merits, by the use of a rigidly scientific method; and only if they are established as true may they be allowed to control the emotional and volitional life.

For this method of approach, as will be clear from all that has been said in the preceding exposition, we have the warmest sympathy; indeed, we believe, there is nothing wrong with the method itself, so far as it goes, but the trouble lies in the application of the method. If a man were truly scientific, we think, he would be convinced of the truth of Christianity whether he were a saint or a demon; since the truth of Christianity does not at all depend upon the state of the soul of the investigator, but is objectively fixed. But the question is whether a method which ignores the consciousness of sin is really scientific or not; and the answer must be, we think, that it is not. If you take account of all the facts, you will be convinced of the truth of Christianity; but you cannot take account of all the facts if you ignore the fact of sin. You cannot

take account of all the facts if, while searching the
heavens above and the earth beneath, you neglect the
facts of your own soul.

Let us see how the ostensibly scientific approach to
Christianity works out.   In pursuance of it we begin
in a systematic way; we bring forward, first, our arguments for the existence of a personal God.   And I
for my part believe that they are rather good arguments; they have not altogether been demolished, I
think, by the criticism of Kant.   If, then, we have
established the existence of God, the question arises
whether He has revealed Himself in such fashion as
that personal communion with Him becomes possible
for mankind.   Probably it will be admitted that if
He has done so at all, He has done so in the Christian
religion; Christianity will probably be admitted to offer
the most plausible claim, at least, among all the religions of the world to be based upon a real revelation
of God.   But has even the Christian claim accredited
itself?   It has done so—to put the matter in briefest
compass and deal with it at the really crucial point—
if Jesus rose from the dead; it has not done so if He
did not rise.   Now there is certainly some evidence for
the resurrection of Jesus.   Admittedly His intimate
friends believed that He had risen, and upon that belief the Church was founded.   But what in turn caused
that belief?   Many answers have been proposed to this
question; but none of them is thoroughly satisfactory,
except the simple answer that the belief of the disciples
was founded upon fact.   So much will be rather widely
admitted; the origin of the Christian Church is

admittedly a very puzzling fact; only ignorance can deny the difficulty of the historical problem that it involves for all naturalistic historians.

But a difficulty, it will be said, is also found in the traditional solution, as well as in the naturalistic solutions. The difficulty appears in the supernatural character of the alleged event. If the resurrection were an ordinary event, the evidence for it would admittedly be sufficient; but then as a matter of fact it is not an ordinary event but a miracle, and against the acceptance of any such thing there is an enormous weight of presumption.

This objection I for my part am not at all inclined to take lightly. Indeed, if the evidence for the resurrection, as we have outlined it, stood alone, it might, I think, be insufficient. Even if a dozen men for whose character and attainments I had the highest respect were to come into the room and tell me, quite independently, that they had seen a man rise from the dead, I am not sure whether I should believe them for a moment. Why, then, do I accord to witnesses of so long ago—witnesses too, who lived in a comparatively unscientific age (though its unscientific character is often enormously exaggerated)—a degree of credence which I might refuse to trained observers of the present day? Why do I believe in the resurrection of Jesus when I might not believe, even on the basis of overwhelming testimony, in the resurrection of one of my contemporaries?

The question seems at first sight hard to answer, but the answer is really not so difficult as it seems. The answer is that I believe in the miracle which is at the

foundation of the Christian Church because in that case
the question does not concern merely the resurrection
of a person about whom I know nothing, a mere x or y,
but it concerns specifically the resurrection of Jesus; and
Jesus was like no person who has ever lived.   It is unbelievable, I say, that any ordinary man should be
raised from the dead, but then Jesus was no ordinary
man; in His case the enormous presumption against
miracle is reversed; in His case, far from its being inconceivable that He should have been raised, it is inconceivable that He should not have been raised; such an
one as He could not possibly have been holden of
death.   Thus the direct evidence for the resurrection
is supplemented by an impression of the moral uniqueness of Jesus' person.   That does not mean that if
we are impressed by the moral uniqueness of Jesus' person, the direct evidence for the resurrection is unnecessary, or that the Christian can be indifferent to it; but
it does mean that that impression must be added to the
direct evidence in order to produce conviction.

But how do we know that Jesus' moral character is
absolutely unique?   We do so only because of our conviction of sin.   Convinced of our own impurity, as revealed by the majesty of the divine law, we become convinced of His dissimilarity in kind from us, and thus
we say that He alone was pure.   Thus even in order to
establish the fact of the resurrection, the lesson of the
law must be learned.

In another way also the conviction of sin is necessary in order that we may believe in the resurrection of
Christ and thus accept the claims of Christianity.   The

resurrection, as we have seen, if it really took place, was a miracle; it involved an intrusion of the creative power of God into the course of the world. So stupendous an event is difficult to accept unless we can detect for it an adequate purpose; and the adequate purpose is detected only by the man who is under conviction of sin. Such a man alone can understand the need of redemption; he alone knows that sin has introduced a great rent into the very structure of the universe, which only a creative act of God can close. The truly penitent man rejoices in the supernatural; for he knows that nothing natural can possibly meet his need. He rejoices even in the new consciousness of the uniformity and unity of nature which has been so widely disseminated by modern science; for that uniformity of nature only reveals with new clearness the sheer uniqueness of the redemption offered by Christ.

Thus even in order to exhibit the truth of Christianity at the bar of reason, it is necessary to learn the lesson of the law. It is impossible to prove first that Christianity is true, and then proceed on the basis of its truth to become conscious of one's sin; for the fact of sin is itself one of the chief foundations upon which the proof is based.

When that fact of sin is recognized, and when to the recognition of it is added a fair scrutiny of the historical evidence, then it seems thoroughly reasonable to believe that Christianity is true. Anyone whose mind is clear, no matter what his personal attitude may be, will, we think, accept the truth of Christianity; but no one's mind is clear who denies the facts of his own soul: in order to come to the Christian view of Christ it is necessary only to be scientific; but no one can be truly scientific who ignores the fact of sin.

We are not ignoring the emotional and volitional aspects of faith; we are not denying that as a matter of fact, in humanity as it is actually constituted, an intellectual conviction of the truth of Christianity is always accompanied by a change of heart and a new direction for the will. That does not mean that Christianity is true only for those who thus will to accept it, and that it is not true for others; on the contrary it is true, we think, even for the demons in hell as well as for the saints in heaven, though its truth does the demons no good. But for a thing to be true is one thing and for it to be recognized as true is another; and in order that Christianity may be recognized as true by men upon this earth the blinding effects of sin must be removed. The blinding effects of sin are removed by the Spirit of God; and the Spirit chooses to do that only for those whom He brings by the new birth into the Kingdom of God. Regeneration, or the new birth, therefore, does not stand in opposition to a truly scientific attitude toward the evidence, but on the contrary it is necessary in order that that truly scientific attitude may be attained; it is not a substitute for the intellect, but on the contrary by it the intellect is made to be a trustworthy instrument for apprehending truth. The true state of the case appears in the comprehensive answer of the Westminster *Shorter Catechism* to the question, "What is effectual calling?" "Effectual calling," says the Catechism, "is the work of God's Spirit, where-

by, convincing us of our sin and misery, enlightening
our minds in the knowledge of Christ, and renewing
our wills, He doth persuade and enable us to embrace
Jesus Christ, freely offered to us in the gospel." That
does justice to all aspects of the matter; conviction of
sin and misery as the prerequisite of faith, the enlightening of a mind blinded by sin, the renewing of the
will; and all these things produced by the Spirit of God.

In the second place, instead of following the purely
intellectual way that has just been discussed, men sometimes try to come to Christ through the sense of beauty.
And indeed it is a beautiful thing—this life of Christ
rising like a fair flower amid the foulness of the Roman
Empire, this strange teaching so simple and yet so profound. But there is at least one objection to the sense
of beauty as the way of approach to Christ—it cannot
be forced upon those who desire it not. There is no disputing about tastes: one man may admire Jesus, another may prefer the pagan glories of ancient Greece or
of the Italian Renaissance; and if it is a merely esthetic
question, no universally valid decision can be attained.
If the way of approach is merely through the sense of
beauty, then the universality of the Christian religion,
at any rate, must be given up.

Is the life and teaching of Jesus, moreover, so beautiful after all? Jesus said some things that offend the
sensibilities of many people, as when He spoke of the
outer darkness and the everlasting fire, and of the sin
that shall not be forgiven either in this world or in that
which is to come. These things cannot be called exactly
"pretty"; and by many men they are simply ignored.

Some years ago I heard a preacher who, after the customary abuse of Calvin and others, obtained a smile from his congregation by quoting something that Cotton Mather had said about hell. The question that might have occurred to me as I listened was why the preacher had to go so far afield. Why should he have had recourse to Cotton Mather, when Jesus would have done just as well? There are words of Jesus about hell, just as terrible as any that can be found in the writings of the theologians; and those words might have obtained as good a smile—from that congregation—as the words of Jonathan Edwards or Cotton Mather or the rest.

There is, however, one class of persons from whom those words would have obtained no such smile, and to whom they would have seemed not to mar one whit the beauty of the teaching of our Lord. These are the persons who have passed through the strange experience of the conviction of sin, the persons who hold the same view of sin and retribution that Jesus held. To such persons, and to such persons alone, the beauty of Jesus is without a flaw. That beauty cannot be appreciated without a knowledge of the holiness upon which it is based; and the holiness is unknown except to those who have been convicted of their own sin through learning the lesson of the law.

In the third place, men try to come to Christ through the desire for companionship; they seek in Him a friend who will be faithful when other friends depart. But companionship with Jesus is not always the comfortable thing that it is sometimes thought to be; Jesus did not always make it easy to be a disciple of Him.

"Let the dead bury their dead," He told the enthusiast who came eagerly to Him but was not willing at once to forsake all. "One thing thou lackest," He said to the rich young ruler, and the young man went sorrowing away. "He that is not with me," He said to men who wanted to enjoy His companionship without definitely taking sides, "is against me." "If any man come to me, and hate not his father, and mother, and wife, and children . . . . he cannot be my disciple." It was a very serious thing, in those Galilean days, to be a disciple of Christ.

And it was a serious thing not only in the sphere of conduct but also in the sphere of thought. There could be no greater mistake than to suppose that a man in those days could *think* as he liked and still be a follower of Jesus. On the contrary the offence lay just as much in the sphere of doctrine as in the sphere of life; the exclusive claims of Jesus—that a man should if necessary forsake all to follow Him—were grounded in the stupendous view which He held of His own Person and mission; no man could really enjoy the companionship of Jesus who did not admit His absolute sway.

There were some indeed to whom His yoke was easy and His burden was light; there were some who rejoiced in His lofty demands as the very hope of their lives. These were the men who had come under the conviction of sin—the sinners, who without a plea except in His mercy heard the gracious words, "Thy sins are forgiven thee."

As it was then, so also it will be today: the companionship of Jesus is indeed a gracious thing for burdened souls; but it is a terrible thing for those who have any trust in a righteousness of their own. No man can call Jesus friend who does not also call Him Lord; and no man can call Him Lord who could not say first: "Depart from me; for I am a sinful man, O Lord." At the root of all true companionship with Jesus, therefore, is the consciousness of sin and with it the reliance upon His mercy; to have fellowship with Him it is necessary to learn the terrible lesson of God's law.

Finally, men seek to come to Christ through the desire for a worthy ideal; indeed that way is just now the most commonly followed of all. "I may not be very orthodox," says many a modern man, "but I am a Christian because I believe that the principles of Jesus will solve all the problems of my life and also all the problems of society."

The most obvious objection to this way of approach to Jesus is that it will not work; an ideal is quite powerless to a man who is under the thraldom of sin; and the real glory of Jesus is that He breaks that thraldom, and instead of giving merely guidance, as an ideal would do, gives also power.

There is, however, also another objection. Jesus, it is said, can be taken as the supreme and perfect ideal for humanity. But is He really a perfect ideal? There is one difficulty which modern men find about taking Him as such—the difficulty due to His stupendous claims. There can be no real doubt, in the mind of a historian who examines the facts, but that Jesus of Nazareth regarded Himself as the Messiah; and there can also be no real doubt but that He regarded Himself as the Messiah not merely in some lower meaning of the term, but in the lofty meaning by which it designated the heavenly Son of Man, the glorious figure who appears in the seventh chapter of Daniel in the presence of the Ancient of Days. This Jesus of Nazareth, in other words, who is to be taken as the supreme moral ideal of the race, actually believed, as He looked out upon His contemporaries, that He was one day to sit upon the throne of God and be their Judge and the Judge of all the earth! Would not such a person have been, if not actually insane, at least unbalanced and unworthy of the full confidence of men?

There is only one way of overcoming this difficulty —it is to accept the lofty claims of Jesus as sober truth. If the claims are denied, then—argue as men will—the Galilean prophet ceases to be a supreme and perfect ideal. But the claims can be accepted as true only when one takes the same view of Jesus' mission as that which Jesus took, only when one regards Him as the divine Redeemer who came voluntarily into the world to save mankind from the guilt and power of sin. If Jesus is only an ideal, He is not a perfect ideal; for He claimed to be far more: but if He is the Saviour from sin, then He is the perfect Example that can never be surpassed. But He can be accepted as the Saviour from sin only by those who hold the same view of sin as that which He held; and that view can be held only by those who have learned the lesson of the law.

The fact is, then, that there is no other way of coming to Christ except the old, old way that is found in the conviction of sin. The truth of Christianity cannot be established by the intellect unless an important part of the argument is based upon the fact of sin which is revealed by the law of God; the beauty of Jesus, which attracts the gaze of men, cannot be appreciated without a knowledge of the holiness upon which it is based; the companionship of Jesus is possible only to those who say first, in deep contrition: "Depart from me; for I am a sinful man, O Lord"; the example of Jesus is powerless to those who are in the bondage of evil habit, and it is not even a perfect example unless He be the divine Redeemer that He claimed to be. The true schoolmaster to bring men to Christ is found, therefore, now and always in the law of God—the law of God that gives to men the consciousness of sin.

A new and more powerful proclamation of that law is perhaps the most pressing need of the hour; men would have little difficulty with the gospel if they had only learned the lesson of the law. As it is, they are turning aside from the Christian pathway; they are turning to the village of Morality, and to the house of Mr. Legality, who is reported to be very skillful in relieving men of their burdens. Mr. Legality has indeed in our day disguised himself somewhat, but he is the same deceiver as the one of whom Bunyan wrote. "Making Christ Master" in the life, putting into practice "the principles of Christ" by one's own efforts— these are merely new ways of earning salvation by one's own obedience to God's commands. And they are undertaken because of a lax view of what those commands are. So it always is: a low view of law always brings legalism in religion; a high view of law makes a man a seeker after grace. Pray God that the high view may again prevail; that Mount Sinai may again overhang the path and shoot forth flames, in order that then the men of our time may, like Christian in the allegory, meet some true Evangelist, who shall point them out the old, old way, through the little wicket gate, to the place somewhat ascending where they shall really see the Cross and the figure of Him that did hang thereon, that at that sight the burden of the guilt of sin, which no human hand could remove, may fall from their back into a sepulchre beside the way, and that then, with wondrous lightness and freedom and joy, they may walk the Christian path, through the Valley of Humiliation and the Valley of the Shadow of Death, and up over the Delectable Mountains, until at last they pass triumphant across the river into the City of God.

CHAPTER V

FAITH AND THE GOSPEL

If what we have said so far be correct, there is now living a Saviour who is worthy of our trust, even Christ Jesus the Lord, and a deadly need of our souls for which we come to Him, namely, the curse of God's law, the terrible guilt of sin. But these things are not all that is needed in order that we may have faith. It is also necessary that there should be contact between the Saviour and our need. Christ is a sufficient Saviour; but what has He done, and what will He do, not merely for the men who were with Him in the days of His flesh, but for us? How is it that Christ touches our lives?

The answer which the Word of God gives to that question is perfectly specific and perfectly plain. Christ touches our lives, according to the New Testament, through the Cross. We deserved eternal death, in accordance with the curse of God's law; but the Lord Jesus, because He loved us, took upon Himself the guilt of our sins and died instead of us on Calvary. And faith consists simply in our acceptance of that wondrous gift. When we accept the gift, we are clothed, entirely without merit of our own, by the righteousness of Christ; when God looks upon us, He sees not our impurity but the spotless purity of Christ, and accepts us "as righteous in His sight, only for the righteousness of Christ imputed to us, and received by faith alone."

That view of the Cross, it cannot be denied, runs counter to the mind of the natural man. It is not, indeed, complicated or obscure; on the contrary it is so simple that a child can understand, and what is really obscure is the manifold modern effort to explain the Cross away in such fashion as to make it more agreeable to human pride. But certainly it is mysterious, and certainly it demands for its acceptance a tremendous sense of sin and guilt. That sense of sin and guilt, that moral awakening of a soul dead in sin, is the work of the Spirit of God; without the Spirit of God no human persuasion will ever bring men to faith. But that does not mean that we should be careless about the way in which we proclaim the gospel: because the proclamation of the message is insufficient to induce faith, it does not follow that it is unnecessary; on the contrary it is the means which the Spirit Himself graciously uses in bringing men to Christ. Every effort, therefore, should be made, with the help of God, to remove objections to this "word of the Cross" and to present it in all its gracious power.

No systematic effort can indeed here be made to deal with the objections.[1] All that can be done is to mention one or two of them, in order that our present point, that the Cross of Christ is the special basis of Christian faith, may become plain.

In the first place, then, the view of the Cross which has just been outlined is often belittled as being merely

---

[1] Some of them have been dealt with briefly in *Christianity and Liberalism*, 1923, pp. 120-136.

a "theory of the atonement." We can have the fact of the atonement, it is said, no matter what particular theory of it we hold, and indeed even without holding any particular theory of it at all. So this substitutionary view, it is said, is after all only one theory among many.

This objection is based upon a mistaken view of the distinction between fact and theory, and upon a somewhat ambiguous use of the word "theory." What is meant by a "theory"? Undoubtedly the word often has rather an unfavorable sound; and the use of it in the present connection might seem to imply that the view of the atonement which is designated as a "theory" is a mere effort of man to explain in his own way what God has given. But might not God have revealed the "theory" of a thing just as truly as the thing itself; might He not Himself have given the explanation when He gave the thing? In that case the explanation just as much as the thing itself comes to us with a divine authority, and it is impossible to accept one without accepting the other.

We have not yet, however, quite gotten to the heart of the matter. Men say that they accept the fact of the atonement without accepting the substitutionary theory of it, and indeed without being sure of any theory of it at all. The trouble with this attitude is that the moment we say "atonement" we have already overstepped the line that separates fact from theory; an "atonement" even in the most general and most indefinite sense that could conceivably be given to the word, cannot possibly be a mere fact, but is a fact as explained by its purpose and results. If we say that an event was an "atonement" for sin or an "atonement" in the sense of an establishment of harmony between God and man, we have done more than designate the mere external event. What we have really done is to designate the event with an explanation of its meaning. So the atonement wrought by Christ can never be a bare fact, in the sense with which we are now dealing. The bare fact is simply the death of a Jew upon a cross in the first century of our era, and that bare fact is entirely without value to anyone; what gives it its value is the explanation of it as a means by which sinful man was brought into the presence of God. It is impossible for us to obtain the slightest benefit from a mere contemplation of the death of Christ; all the benefit comes from our knowledge of the meaning of that death, or in other words (if the term be used in a high sense) from our "theory" of it. If, therefore, we speak of the bare "fact" of the atonement, as distinguished from the "theory" of it, we are indulging in a misleading use of words; the bare fact is the death, and the moment we say "atonement" we have committed ourselves to a theory. The important thing, then, is, since we must have some theory, that the particular theory that we hold shall be correct.

But, it may be said, might not God really have accomplished some wonderful thing by the death of Christ without revealing to us, except in the most general terms, what it was? Might He not have told us simply that our salvation depends upon the death of Christ without at all telling us why that is so? We

answer that He certainly might have done so; but the
question is whether He has actually done so. There
are many things which He might conceivably have done
and yet has not actually done. Conceivably, for example, He might have saved us by placing us in a condition of unconsciousness and then awakening us to a
new life in which sin should have no place. But it is
perfectly plain that as a matter of fact He has not done
so; and even we, with our poor finite intelligence, may
perhaps see that His way is better than that. So it is
perfectly conceivable that He might have saved us by
the death of Christ without revealing to us how He
did so; in that case we should have to prostrate ourselves before a crucifix with an understanding far lower
than that which is found in the lowest forms of Roman
Catholic piety. He might conceivably have treated us
thus. But, thank God, He has not done so; thank
God He has been pleased, in His infinite grace, to deal
with us not as with sticks and stones, but as with persons; thank God He has been pleased to reveal to us
in the Cross of Christ a meaning that stills the despairing voice of conscience and puts in our hearts a song of
joy that shall resound to His praise so long as eternity
endures.

That richness of meaning is found only in the blessed
doctrine that upon the Cross the Lord took our place,
that He offered Himself "a sacrifice to satisfy divine
justice, and reconcile us to God." There are indeed
other ways of contemplating the Cross, and they should
certainly not be neglected by the Christian man. But
it is a sad and fatal mistake to treat those other ways

as though they lay on the same plane with this one
fundamental way; in reality the other "theories" of
the atonement lose all their meaning unless they are
taken in connection with this one blessed "theory."
When taken with this way of looking upon the Cross,
the other ways are full of helpfulness to the Christian
man; but without it they lead only to confusion and
despair.   Thus the Cross of Christ is certainly a noble
example of self-sacrifice; but if it be only a noble example of self-sacrifice, it has no comfort for burdened
souls; it certainly shows how God hates sin; but if it
does nothing but show how God hates sin, it only
deepens our despair; it certainly exhibits the love of
God, but if it does nothing but exhibit the love of God
it is a mere meaningless exhibition which seems unworthy of God.   Many things are taught us by the
Cross; but the other things are taught us only if the
really central meaning is preserved, the central meaning
upon which all the rest depends.   On the cross the
penalty of our sins was paid; it is as though we ourselves had died in fulfillment of the just curse of the
law; the handwriting of ordinances that was against
us was wiped out; and henceforth we have an entirely
new life in the full favor of God.

There is, however, another objection to this "word
of the Cross."   The objection comes from those who
place faith in a person in opposition to acceptance of a
doctrine, especially a doctrine that is based upon what
happened long ago.   Can we not, it is said, trust Christ
as a present Saviour without accepting a doctrine that
explains the death that He died in the first century of

our era? This question, in one form or another, is often asked, and it is often answered in the affirmative. Indeed, the doctrinal message about Christ is often represented as a barrier that needs to be done away in order that we may have Christ Himself; faith in a doctrine should be removed, it is said, in order that faith in a Person may remain.

Whatever estimate may finally be made of this way of thinking, it must at any rate be admitted at the start that it involves a complete break with the primitive Christian Church. If any one thing must be clear to the historian, it is that Christianity at the beginning was founded squarely upon an account of things that had happened, upon a piece of news, or in other words, upon a "gospel." The matter is particularly clear in the summary which Paul in I Cor. xv. 3-7 gives of the primitive Jerusalem tradition: "How that Christ died for our sins according to the Scriptures; and that he was buried, and that he rose again the third day according to the Scriptures." The earliest Christian Church in Jerusalem clearly was founded not merely upon what always was true but upon things that had happened, not merely upon eternal truths of religion but upon historical facts. The historical facts upon which it was founded were, moreover, not bare facts but facts that had a meaning; it was not only said that "Christ died" —that would be (at least if the word "Christ" were taken as a mere proper name and not in the full, lofty signification of "Messiah") a bare fact—but it was said "Christ died for our sins," and that was a fact with the meaning of the fact—in other words it was a doctrine.

This passage is of course not isolated in the New Testament teaching, but is merely a summary of what is really the presupposition of the whole. Certainly the grounding of Christianity upon historical facts, upon events as distinguished from mere eternal principles, cannot be regarded as a point in which the apostolic Church was in contradiction to the teaching which Jesus Himself gave in the days of His flesh, but finds it justification in the words which Jesus uttered. Of course if Jesus really, as the New Testament books all represent, came—to use the language of a certain distinguished preacher—not primarily to say something but to do something, and if that something was done by His death and resurrection, then it is natural that the full explanation of what was done could not be given until the death and resurrection had occurred. It is a great mistake, therefore, to regard the Sermon on the Mount as somehow more sacred or more necessary to the nurture of the Christian life than, for example, the eighth chapter of Romans. But although the full explanation of redemption could not be given until the redeeming event had taken place, yet our Lord did, by way of prophecy, even in the days of His flesh, point forward to what was to come. He did point forward to catastrophic events by which salvation was to be given to men; all efforts to eliminate this element in His teaching about the Kingdom of God have failed. During Jesus' earthly ministry the redeeming work which the Old Testament prophets had predicted was still in the future; to the apostolic Church it was in the past: but both Jesus and the apostolic Church did proclaim, the one by way of prophecy, the other by way of historical testimony, an event upon which the hopes of believers were based.

Thus the notion that insistence upon the message of redemption through the death and resurrection of our Lord places a barrier between ourselves and Him was not shared by the earliest Christian Church; on the contrary, in the apostolic age that message was regarded as the source of all light and joy. And in the present instance, as in so many other instances, it can be shown that the apostles (and our Lord Himself) were right. The truth is that the whole opposition between faith in a person and acceptance of a message about the person must be given up. It is based, as we have already seen, upon a false psychology; a person cannot be trusted without acceptance of the facts about the person. But in the case of Jesus the notion is particularly false; for it is just the message about Jesus, the message that sets forth his Cross and resurrection, that brings us into contact with Him. Without that message He would be forever remote—a great Person, but one with whom we could have no communion—but through that message He comes to be our Saviour. True communion with Christ comes not when a man merely says, in contemplating the Cross, "This was a righteous man," or "This was a son of God," but when he says with tears of gratitude and joy, "He loved me and gave Himself for me."

There is a wonderful clause in the Westminster

Shorter Catechism which puts the true state of the case in classic form. "Faith in Jesus Christ," says the Catechism, "is a saving grace, whereby we receive and rest upon Him alone for salvation, *as He is offered to us in the gospel.*" In that last clause, "as He is offered to us in the gospel," we have the centre and core of the whole matter. The Lord Jesus Christ does us no good, no matter how great He may be, unless He is offered to us; and as a matter of fact He is offered to us in the good news of His redeeming work. There are other conceivable ways in which He might have been offered to us; but this has the advantage of being God's way. And I rather think that in the long run we may come to see that God's way is best.

At the beginning, it is true, there may be much that we cannot understand; there are things about the way of salvation that we may at first have to take in the fullest sense "on faith." The greatest offence of all, perhaps, is the wondrous simplicity of the gospel, which is so different from the plans which we on our part had made. Like Naaman the Syrian we are surprised when our rich fees and our letters of introduction are spurned, when all our efforts to save ourselves by our own character or our own good works are counted as not of the slightest avail. "Are not Abana and Pharpar, rivers of Damascus," we say, "better than all the waters of Israel?" Are not our own efforts to put into operation the "principles of Jesus," or to "make Christ Master" by our own efforts in our lives, better than this strange message of the Cross? But like Naaman we may find, if we put away our pride, if we are willing to take God at His word, if we confess that His way is best, that our flesh, so foul with sin, may come again like the flesh of a little child and we may be clean.

And then will be revealed to us the fuller wonders of salvation; then, as the years go by, we shall come to understand ever more and more the glory of the Cross. It may seem strange at first that Christ should be offered to us not in some other way, but so specifically in this way; but as we grow in knowledge and in grace we shall come to see with increasing fullness that no way could possibly be better than this. Christ is offered to us not in general, but "in the gospel"; but in the gospel there is included all that the heart of man can wish.

We ought never, therefore, to set present communion with Christ, as so many are doing, in opposition to the gospel; we ought never to say that we are interested in what Christ does for us now, but are not so much interested in what He did long ago. Do you know what soon happens when men talk in that way? The answer is only too plain. They soon lose all contact with the real Christ; what they call "Christ" in the soul soon comes to have little to do with the actual person, Jesus of Nazareth; their religion would really remain essentially the same if scientific history should prove that such a person as Jesus never lived. In other words, they soon came to substitute the imaginings of their own hearts for what God has revealed; they substitute mysticism for Christianity as the religion of their souls.

That danger should be avoided by the Christian man with all his might and main. God has given us an

anchor for our souls; He has anchored us to Himself
by the message of the Cross. Let us never cast that
anchor off; let us never weaken our connection with
the events upon which our faith is based. Such de-
pendence upon the past will never prevent us from having present communion with Christ; our communion
with Him will be as inward, as intimate, as untram-
melled by any barriers of sense, as the communion of
which the mystics boast; but unlike the communion of
the mystics it will be communion not with the imaginings of our own hearts, but with the real Saviour Jesus
Christ. The gospel of redemption through the Cross
and resurrection of Christ is not a barrier between us
and Christ, but it is the blessed tie, by which, with the
cords of His love, He has bound us forever to Him.

Acceptance of the Lord Jesus Christ, as He is offered
to us in the gospel of His redeeming work, is saving
faith. Despairing of any salvation to be obtained by
our own efforts, we simply trust in Him to save us;
we say no longer, as we contemplate the Cross, merely
"He saved others" or "He saved the world" or "He
saved the Church"; but we say, every one of us, by the
strange individualizing power of faith, "He loved *me*
and gave Himself for *me*." When a man once says
that, in his heart and not merely with his lips, then no
matter what his guilt may be, no matter how far he
is beyond any human pale, no matter how little opportunity he has for making good the evil that he has
done, he is a ransomed soul, a child of God forever.

At this point, a question may perhaps be asked. We
have said that saving faith is acceptance of Christ, not

merely in general, but as He is offered to us in the gospel. How much, then, of the gospel, it may be asked, does a man need to accept in order that he may be saved; what, to put it baldly, are the minimum doctrinal requirements in order that a man may be a Christian? That is a question which, in one form or another, I am often asked; but it is also a question which I have never answered, and which I have not the slightest intention of answering now. Indeed it is a question which I think no human being can answer. Who can presume to say for certain what is the condition of another man's soul; who can presume to say whether the other man's attitude toward Christ, which he can express but badly in words, is an attitude of saving faith or not? This is one of the things which must surely be left to God.

There is indeed a certain reason why it is natural to ask the question to which we have just referred; it is natural because of the existence of a visible Church. The visible Church should strive to receive, into a communion for prayer and fellowship and labor, as many as possible of those who are united to Christ in saving faith, and it should strive to exclude as many as possible of those who are not so united to Him. If it does not practise exclusion as well as inclusion, it will soon come to stand for nothing at all, but will be merged in the life of the world; it will soon become like salt that has lost its savour, fit only to be cast out and to be trodden under foot of men.

In order, therefore, that the purity of the Church may be preserved, a confession of faith in Christ must be required of all those who would become Church members. But what kind of confession must it be? I for my part think that it ought to be not merely a verbal confession, but a credible confession. One of the very greatest evils of present-day religious life, it seems to me, is the reception into the Church of persons who merely repeat a form of words such as "I accept Christ as my personal Saviour," without giving the slightest evidence to show that they know what such words mean. As a consequence of this practice, hosts of persons are being received into the Church on the basis, as has been well said, of nothing more than a vague admiration for the moral character of Jesus, or else on the basis of a vague purpose of engaging in humanitarian work. One such person within the Church does more harm to the cause of Christ, I for my part believe, than ten such persons outside; and the whole practice ought to be radically changed. The truth is that the ecclesiastical currency in our day has been sadly debased; Church membership, as well as Church office, no longer means what it ought to mean. In view of such a situation, we ought, I think, to have reality at least; instead of comforting ourselves with columns of church statistics, we ought to face the facts; we ought to recall this paper currency and get back to a standard of gold.

To that end, it should, I think, be made much harder than it now is to enter the Church: the confession of faith that is required should be a credible confession; and if it becomes evident upon examination that a candidate has no notion of what he is doing, he should be advised to enter upon a course of instruction before he becomes a member of the Church. Such a course of instruction, moreover, should be conducted not by comparatively untrained laymen, but ordinarily by the ministers; the excellent institution of the catechetical class should be generally revived. Those churches, like the Lutheran bodies in America, which have maintained that institution, have profited enormously by its employment; and their example deserves to be generally followed.

After all, however, such inquiries into the state of the souls of men and women and children who desire to enter into the Church must be regarded as at the best very rough and altogether provisional. Certainly requirements for Church membership should be distinguished in the sharpest possible way from requirements for the ministry. The confusion of these two things in the ecclesiastical discussions of the past few years has resulted in great injustice to us who are called conservatives in the Church. We have been represented sometimes as though we were requiring an acceptance of the infallibility of Scripture or of the confession of faith of our Church from those who desire to become Church members, whereas in point of fact we have been requiring these things only from candidates for ordination. Surely there is a very important distinction here. Many persons—to take a secular example—can be admitted to an educational institution as students who yet are not qualified for a position in the faculty. Similarly many persons can be admitted to Church membership who yet ought not to be admitted to the ministry; they are qualified to learn, but not qualified to teach; they should not be allowed to stand forth as accredited teachers with the official endorsement of the Church.

This analogy, it is true, does not by any means altogether hold: the Church is not, we think, merely an educational institution, but the visible representative in the world of the body of Christ; and its members are not merely seekers after God, but those who have already found; they are not merely interested in Christ, but are united to Christ by the regenerating act of the Spirit of God. Nevertheless, although the analogy does not fully hold, it does hold far enough to illustrate what we mean. There is a wide margin of difference between qualifications for Church membership and qualifications for office—especially the teaching office that we call the ministry. Many a man, with feeble, struggling belief, torn by many doubts, may be admitted into the fellowship of the Church and of the sacraments; it would be heartless to deprive him of the comfort which such fellowship affords; to such persons the Church freely extends its nurture to the end that they may be led into ever fuller knowledge and ever firmer faith. But to admit such persons to the ministry would be a crime against Christ's little ones, who look to the ministry for an assured word as to the way by which they shall be saved. It is not, however, even such persons to whom chiefly we have reference when we advocate today a greater care in admitting men to the ministry. It is not men who are struggling with doubts and difficulties about the gospel to whose admission we chiefly object, but men who are perfectly satisfied with another gospel; it is not men of ill-assured faith, but men of assured unbelief.

Even with regard to Church membership, as distinguished from the ministry, there is, as we have seen, a limit beyond which exclusion must certainly be practised; not only a desire to enter the Church should be required but also some knowledge of what entering the Church means, not only a confession of faith but a reasonably credible confession. But the point that we are now making is that such requirements ought clearly to be recognized as provisional; they do not determine a man's standing before God, but they only determine, with the best judgment that God has given to feeble and ignorant men, a man's standing in the visible Church. That is one reason why we must refuse to answer, in any definite and formal way, the question as to the minimum doctrinal requirements that are necessary in order that a man may be a Christian.

There is, however, also another reason. The other reason is that the very asking of the question often betokens an unfortunate attitude with regard to Christian truth. For our part we have not much sympathy with the present widespread desire of finding some greatest common denominator which shall unite men of different Christian bodies; for such a greatest common denominator is often found to be very small indeed. Some men seem to devote most of their energies to the task of seeing just how little of Christian truth they can get along with. For our part, we regard it as a perilous business; we prefer, instead of seeing how little of Christian truth we can get along with, to see just how much of Christian truth we can obtain. We ought to search the Scriptures reverently and thoughtfully and pray God that he may lead us into an ever fuller understanding of the truth that can make us wise unto salvation. There is no virtue whatever in ignorance, but much virtue in a knowledge of what God has revealed.

CHAPTER VI

FAITH AND SALVATION

We have been engaging, in the latter part of the last chapter, in something like a digression, and it is time to return to the point at which we left off. When a man, we observed, accepts Christ, not in general but specifically "as He is offered to us in the gospel," such acceptance of Christ is saving faith. It may involve a smaller or a greater amount of knowledge. The greater the amount of knowledge which it involves, the better for the soul; but even a smaller amount of knowledge may bring a true union with Christ. When Christ, as he is offered to us in the gospel of His redeeming work, is thus accepted in faith, the soul of the man who believes is saved.

That salvation of the Christian, in one of its aspects, is called "justification by faith;" and the doctrine of justification by faith must be considered specifically, though briefly, at the present point in our discussion.

There will perhaps, however, be an objection to the terminology that we are venturing to employ. "Justification," it will be said, is a distressingly long word; and as for the word "doctrine," that has a forbidding sound. Instead of such terminology surely we ought to find simpler words which will bring the matter home to modern men in language such as they are accustomed to use.

161

This suggestion is typical of what is often being said at the present time. Many persons are horrified by the use of a theological term; they seem to have a notion that modern Christians must be addressed always in words of one syllable, and that in religion we must abandon the scientific precision of language which is found to be so useful in other spheres. In pursuance of this tendency we have had presented to us recently various translations of the Bible which reduce the Word of God more or less thoroughly to the language of the modern street, or which, as the matter was put recently in my hearing by an intelligent layman, "take all the religion out of the New Testament." But the whole tendency, we for our part think, ought to be resisted. Back of it all seems to lie the strange assumption that modern men, particularly modern university men, can never by any chance learn anything; they do not understand the theological terminology which appears in such richness in the Bible, and that is regarded as the end of the matter; apparently it does not occur to anyone that possibly they might with profit acquire the knowledge of Biblical terminology which now they lack. But I for my part am by no means ready to acquiesce. I am perfectly ready, indeed, to agree that the Bible and the modern man ought to be brought together. But what is not always observed is that there are two ways of attaining that end. One way is to bring the Bible down to the level of the modern man; but the other way is to bring the modern man up to the level of the Bible. For my part, I am inclined to advocate the latter way. And I am by no means ready to relinquish the advantages of a precise terminology in summarizing Bible truth. In religion as well as in other spheres a precise terminology is mentally economical in the end; it repays amply the slight effort required for the mastery of it. Thus I am not at all ashamed to speak, even in this day and generation, of "the doctrine of justification by faith."

It should not be supposed, however, that that doctrine is an abstruse or intricate thing. On the contrary it is a very simple thing, and it is instinct with life.

It is an answer to the greatest personal question ever asked by a human soul—the question: "How shall I be right with God; how do I stand in God's sight; with what favor does He look upon me?" There are those, it must be admitted, who never raise that question; there are those who are concerned with the question of their standing before men, but never with the question of their standing before God; there are those who are interested in what "people say," but not in the question what God says. Such men, however, are not those who move the world; they are apt to go with the current; they are apt to do as others do; they are not the heroes who change the destinies of the race. The beginning of true nobility comes when a man ceases to be interested in the judgment of men, and becomes interested in the judgment of God.

But if we can gain that much insight, if we have become interested in the judgment of God, how shall we stand in that judgment? How shall we become right with God? The most obvious answer is: "By obeying the law of God, by being what God wants us to be." There is absolutely nothing wrong in theory about that answer; the only trouble is that for us it does not work. If we had obeyed the law of God, if we were what God wants us to be, all would no doubt be well; we could approach the judgment seat of God and rely simply upon His just recognition of the facts. But, alas, we have not obeyed God's law, but have transgressed it in thought, word and deed; and far from being what God wants us to be, we are stained and soiled with sin. The stain is not merely on the surface; it is not a thing that can easily be wiped off; but it permeates the recesses of our souls. And the clearer be our understanding of God's law, the deeper becomes our despair. Some men seek a refuge from condemnation in a low view of the law of God; they limit the law to external commands, and by obeying those commands they hope to buy God's favor. But the moment a man gains a vision of the law as it is—especially as it is revealed in the words and example of Jesus—at that moment he knows that he is undone. If our being right with God depends upon anything that is in us, we are without hope.

Another way, however, has been opened into God's presence; and the opening of that way is set forth in the gospel. We deserved eternal death; we deserved exclusion from the household of God; but the Lord Jesus took upon Himself all the guilt of our sins and died instead of us on the cross. Henceforth the law's demands have been satisfied for us by Christ, its terror for us is gone, and clothed no longer in our righteousness but in the righteousness of Christ we stand without fear, as Christ would stand without fear, before the judgment seat of God. Men say that that is an intricate theory; but surely the adjective is misplaced. It is mysterious, but it is not intricate; it is wonderful, but it is so simple that a child can understand.

Two objections to the doctrine of justification, however, need to be considered even in a brief presentation such as that in which we are now engaged.

In the first place, it is said, "justification" is a "forensic" term; it is borrowed, that is, from the law-courts; it smells of musty volumes bound in legal calf; and we moderns prefer other sources for our figures of speech; we prefer to conceive of salvation in a vital, rather than in a legal, way.

In answer it may be said, of course, that justification by faith is by no means all of the Christian doctrine of salvation; it has as its other side the doctrine of regeneration or the new birth. What the Christian has from God is not merely a new and right relation to Him in which the guilt of sin is wiped out, but also a new life in which the power of sin is broken; the Christian view of salvation is vital as well as forensic. This modern way of thinking, on the other hand, errs in being one-sided; it errs, not indeed in insisting upon the "vital" aspect of salvation, but in maintaining that salvation is only vital. When the vital aspect of salvation is thus separated from the forensic aspect, the consequences are serious indeed; what really happens is that the whole ethical character of Christianity is endangered or destroyed. It is important to understand that the Christian has a new life in addition to a new standing before the judgment seat of God; but to be interested in the new life to the exclusion of the new standing before God is to deprive the new life of its moral significance. For it is only as judged in accordance with some absolute norm of righteousness that that new life differs from the life of plants or beasts.

The ultimate question, however, that is involved in the objection concerns the validity of retributive justice. The objection regards as derogatory to the doctrine of justification the fact that it uses the language of the law-courts. But is that fact really derogatory to the doctrine? We for our part think that it is not, for the simple reason that we hold a totally different view of the law-courts from the view that the objector holds. At this point, as at so many other points, there is revealed the far-reaching character of the disagreement in the modern religious world. The disagreement concerns not merely what is ordinarily called religion, but it concerns almost every department of human life. In particular it concerns the underlying theory of human justice.

The objector regards as derogatory the fact that our doctrine of justification uses the language of the law-courts. But he does so only because of the limited function with which according to his view the law-courts must be content. According to his view our courts of law are concerned only with the reform of the criminal or the protection of society; in connection with our courts he thinks that the whole notion of retributive justice must be given up. Very different is our view; and because it is different, the fact that the doctrine of justification uses legal language appears to us to be not a reproach but a high commendation. Courts, we think, even human courts, far from exercising a merely utilitarian function, are founded upon a principle that is rooted in the very being of God. They do, indeed, also exercise the utilitarian functions of which we have just spoken; they do seek the reform of the criminal and the protection of society: and they must never allow these considerations to be forgotten. But back of all that lies the irreducible fact of retributive justice. We do not mean that human judges can ever speak in any infallible way with the voice of God; human limitations must constantly be borne in mind; a truly just and final settlement must often be left to a higher Assize. But still, when all that and more is admitted, there remains a basis of eternal significance in every true court of law. That significance is, indeed, today often obscured; the low utilitarian theory of which we have just spoken has invaded only too frequently our courtrooms, and put trivial consideration of consequences in place of the majesty of the law. Men are complaining of the result, but are not willing to deal with the cause. They are complaining loudly of the growth of criminality; they are feverishly filling statute books with all sorts of prohibitions: they are trying their best to prevent the disintegration of society. But the whole effort is really quite vain. The real trouble does not lie in the details of our laws, but in the underlying conception of what law is.

Even in the field of detail, it is true, there is room for improvement—improvement in a very different direction, however, from that in which contemporary law-makers are accustomed to turn, improvement in the direction not of increased multiplication of statutes, but of a return to simplicity. Instead of the mass of trivial and often irksome prohibitions which now clog our statute books, legislatures ought to content themselves with what is demanded by the overwhelming moral judgment of the people; one way to encourage respect for law, we think, would be to make law more respectable. The real trouble, however, is more fundamental than all that; it lies, not in matters of detail, but in the underlying principle. Respect for human laws cannot, in the long run, be maintained unless there is such a thing, in the ultimate constitution of things, as justice; mere utilitarianism will never check the rebellion of the flesh; human judges will be respected only when again they are clothed with a majesty which issues ultimately from the law of God.

It is not, therefore, at all derogatory to the doctrine of justification that it uses the language of a court of law; for a court of law represents—in obscure fashion, it is true—a fact in the being of God. Men say indeed that they prefer to conceive of God as a Father rather than as a Judge; but why must the choice be made? The true way to conceive of Him is to conceive of Him both as a Father and as a Judge. Fatherhood, as we know it upon this earth, represents one aspect of God; but to isolate that aspect is to degrade it and deprive it of its ethical quality. Important indeed is the doctrine of the Fatherhood of God; but it would not be important if it were not supplemented by the doctrine of God as the final Judge.

The other objection to the Christian doctrine of justification can be dealt with just as briefly; since the objection, upon examination, soon disappears. Justification, we are told, involves a mere legal trick which is derogatory to the character of God; according to this doctrine, it is said, God is represented as waiting until Christ has paid the price of sin as a substitute for the sinner before He will forgive; He is represented as being bought off by the death of Christ so that He pronounces as righteous in His sight those who are not really righteous at all. "How degrading all that is," the modern man exclaims; "how much better it would be simply to say that God is more willing to forgive than man is willing to be forgiven!" Thus the doctrine of justification is represented as doing despite to the love of God.

This objection ignores a fundamental feature of the doctrine which is being criticized; it ignores the fact that according to the Christan view it is God Himself and not someone else who in the atoning death of Christ pays the price of sin—God Himself in the person of the Son who loved us and gave Himself for us, and God Himself in the person of the Father who so loved the world that He gave His only begotten Son. For us, the Christian holds, salvation is as free as the air we breathe; God's alone the cost, and ours the wondrous gain. Such a view exalts the love of God far more than is ever done by modern theories as to the forgiveness of sin: for those theories are alike in denying, in the last analysis, the dreadful reality and irrevocableness

of guilt; they seek to save the love of God by denying
the moral constitution of His universe, and in doing so
they finally destroy even that which they started out
to conserve; the divine love which they seek to save at
the expense of His justice turns out to be but an easy
complacency which is no love at all. It is misleading to
apply the term "love" to a sentiment that costs nothing.   Very different is the love of which the Bible
speaks; for that love brought the Lord Jesus to the
cross.   The Bible does not hold out hopes to the sinner
by palliating the fact of sin; on the contrary it proclaims
that fact with a terrible earnestness which otherwise has
not been known. But then, on the basis of this ruthless
illumination of the moral facts of life, it provides a full
and complete and absolutely free way of escape through
the sacrifice of Christ.

No doubt that way is not of our own choosing; and
no doubt it may seem strange.   It may seem to be a
strange thing that One should bear the guilt of others'
sins.   And indeed for anyone save Christ that would
have been far beyond even the power of love.   It is perfectly true that one man cannot bear the guilt of another
man's sins; the instances of "vicarious" suffering in
human life, which have been brought to our attention
as being in the same category with the sufferings of
Christ, serve only to show how far the men who adduce
them are from comprehending what is meant by the
Cross.   But because a weak and sinful man cannot bear
the guilt of others' sins, it does not follow that Christ
cannot do so.   And as a matter of fact, thank God, He
has done so; at the Cross the burden of men's sins has

rolled away, and there has come a peace with God that
the world can never know. We are certainly not in-
tending to exalt emotion at the expense of objective
proof; we are opposed with all our might to the substitution of "experience" as the seat of authority in religion for the Word of God: but the Holy Spirit in the
individual soul does bear witness, we think, to the
truthfulness of the Word, and does bear witness to the
saving efficacy of the Cross, when He cries "Abba,
Father" in our hearts. That cry, we think, is a true
echo of the blessed sentence of acquittal, the blessed
"justification," which a sinner receives when Christ is
his advocate at the judgment seat of God.

We have been speaking of "justification." It depends, we have seen, altogether upon the redeeming
work of Christ. But another very important question
remains. If justification depends upon the redeeming
work of Christ, how is the benefit of that redeeming
work applied to the individual soul?

The most natural answer might seem to be that the
soul applies the benefit of Christ's work to itself by its
own appropriation of that work; it might seem natural
to regard the merits of Christ as a sort of fund or store
which can be drawn upon at will by individual men.
But if one thing is clear, it is that such is not the teaching of the Word of God; if one thing is plain, it is that
the New Testament presents salvation, or the entrance
into God's Kingdom, as the work not of man, but of
God and only of God. The redeeming work of Christ
is applied to the individual soul, according to the New
Testament, by the Holy Spirit and by Him alone.

What then do we mean when we speak of "justification *by faith*"?   Faith, after all, is something in man; and therefore if justification depends upon our faith it depends apparently upon us as well as upon God.

The apparent contradiction is welcome; since it leads on to a true conception of faith.   The faith of man, rightly conceived, can never stand in opposition to the completeness with which salvation depends upon God; it can never mean that man does part, while God merely does the rest; for the simple reason that faith consists not in doing something but in receiving something.   To say that we are justified by faith is just another way of saying that we are justified not in slightest measure by ourselves, but simply and solely by the One in whom our faith is reposed.

At this point appears the profound reason for what at first sight might seem to be a surprising fact.   Why is it that with regard to the attainment of salvation the New Testament assigns such an absolutely exclusive place to faith; why does it not also speak, for example, of our being justified by love?   If it did so, it would certainly be more in accord with modern tendencies; indeed, one popular preacher actually asserts that Paul's fundamental doctrine was salvation by love rather than justification by faith.[1]   But of course that only means making the wish the father to the thought; as a matter of fact, whether we like it or not, it is perfectly clear that Paul did not speak of salvation by love, but that he spoke instead of justification by faith.   Surely the thing requires an explanation; and certainly it does

---

[1] Charles E. Jefferson, *The Character of Paul*, 1923, p. 323.

not mean that the apostle was inclined to depreciate love. On the contrary, in one passage he expressly places love ahead of faith. "And now abideth faith, hope, love," he says, "these three; but the greatest of these is love."[2] Why then, if he places love higher, does he attribute, so far as the attainment of salvation is concerned, such an absolutely exclusive place to faith? And why did not Jesus say: "Thy love hath saved thee, go in peace," but rather: "Thy faith hath saved thee"? Why did He say only that to the men and women who came to Him in the days of His flesh; and why does He say only that, in accordance with the whole New Testament, to burdened souls today?

The answer to this question is really abundantly plain. The true reason why faith is given such an exclusive place by the New Testament, so far as the attainment of salvation is concerned, over against love and over against everything else in man except things that can be regarded as mere aspects of faith, is that faith means receiving something, not doing something or even being something. To say, therefore, that our faith saves us means that we do not save ourselves even in slightest measure, but that God saves us. Very different would be the case if our salvation were said to be through love; for then salvation would depend upon a high quality of our own. And that is what the New Testament, above all else, is concerned to deny. The very centre and core of the whole Bible is the doctrine of the grace of God—the grace of God which depends not one whit upon anything that is in man, but is abso-

[2] I Cor. xiii: 13.

lutely undeserved, resistless and sovereign. The theologians of the Church can be placed in an ascending scale according as they have grasped with less or greater clearness that one great central doctrine, that doctrine that gives consistency to all the rest; and Christian experience also depends for its depth and for its power upon the way in which that blessed doctrine is cherished in the depths of the heart. The centre of the Bible, and the centre of Christianity, is found in the grace of God; and the necessary corollary of the grace of God is salvation through faith alone.

We are brought at this point to a profound fact about faith, a fact without which everything else that we have tried to say would be valueless. The fact to which we refer is this: that it is not as a quality of the soul that faith saves a man, but only as the establishment of contact with a real object of the faith.

This fact, in present-day thinking, is generally denied; and from the denial of it proceed many of the evils, intellectual and otherwise, which beset the religious world. Faith is, indeed, nowadays being exalted to the skies; but the sad fact is that this very exaltation of faith is leading logically and inevitably to a bottomless skepticism which is the precursor of despair.

The whole trouble is that faith is being considered merely as a beneficent quality of the soul without respect to the reality or unreality of its object; and the moment faith comes to be considered in that way, in that moment it is destroyed.

Yet at first sight the modern attitude seems to be full of promise; it avoids, for example, the immense difficulty involved in differences of creed. Let a man, it is urged, hold to be true whatever helps him, and let him not interfere with whatever helps his neighbor. What difference does it make, we are asked, what does the work just so the work is done; what difference does it make whether the disease is cured by Christian Science or by simple faith in Christ Jesus? Some people seem to find even bare materialism a helpful doctrine—conducive to a calm and healthy life, preventing morbid fears and nervous strains. If so, why should we unsettle their "faith" by talking about guilt and retribution?

There is unfortunately one great obstacle in the way of such a broad eclecticism. It is a very real obstacle, though at times it seems to be not a bit practical. It is the old obstacle—truth. That was a great scheme of Lessing's *Nathan der Weise*, to let Judaism, Mohammedanism, and Christianity live peacefully side by side, each contributing its quota to the common good of humanity; and the plan has attained enormous popularity since Lessing's day by the admission, to the proposed league of religions, of all the faiths of mankind. But the great trouble is, a creed can be efficient only so long as it is held to be true; if I make my creed effective in my life I can do so only because I regard it as true. But in so doing I am obliged by an inexorable necessity to regard the creed of my neighbor, if it is contradictory to mine, as false. That weakens his faith in his creed, provided he is at all affected by my opinions; he is no longer so sure of the truth of it; and so soon as he is no longer sure of the truth of it, it loses its efficiency. Or if, in deference to my neighbor and the usefulness of his creed, I keep my creed in the background, that tends to weaken my faith in my creed; I come to have the feeling that what must be kept in the dark will not bear the light of day; my creed ceases to be effective in my life. The fact is that all creeds are laying claim to the same thing, namely truth. Consequently, despite all that is said, the creeds, if they are to be held with any fervor, if they are really to have any power, must be opposed to one another; they simply cannot allow one another to work on in peace. If, therefore, we want the work to proceed, we must face and settle this conflict of the means; we cannot call on men's beliefs to help us unless we determine what it is that is to be believed. A faith that can consent to avoid proselytizing among other faiths is not really faith at all.

An objection, however, may remain. What we have said may perhaps sound very logical, and yet it seems to be contradicted by the actual experience of the race. Physicians, for example, are very practical persons; and yet they tell us that faith in very absurd things sometimes brings beneficent .and far-reaching results. If, therefore, faith in such diverse and contradictory things brings results, if it relieves the distresses of suffering humanity, how can we have the heart to insist on logical consistency in the things that are believed? On the contrary, it is urged, let us be satisfied with any kind of faith just so it does the work; it makes no difference what is believed just so the healthgiving attitude of faith is there; the less dogmatic faith is, the purer it is, because it is the less weakened by the dangerous alloy of knowledge.

It is perfectly clear that such an employment of faith is bringing results. But the curious thing is that if faith be employed in this particular way it is always employment of the faith of other people that brings the results, and never employment of one's own faith. For the man who can speak in this way is himself always not a believer but a skeptic. The basal fact about faith is that all faith has an object; all faith is not only possessed by someone, but it consists in confidence *in* someone. An outsider may not think that it is really the object that does the work; from his scientific vantage ground, he may see clearly that it is just the faith itself, considered merely as a psychological phenomenon, that is the important thing, and that any other object would have answered as well. But the one who does the believing is always convinced just exactly that it is *not* the faith but the object which is helping him; the moment he becomes convinced that the object was not really important and that it was really just his own faith that was helping him, at that moment his faith disappears. It was that previous false belief, then—the belief that it was the object and not the faith that was doing the work—it was that false belief that helped him.

Now things that are false will apparently do some rather useful things. If we may be permitted to use again, and to apply a little further, an illustration that we have already used in a different connection,[3] it may be remarked that a counterfeit note will buy many useful commodities—until it is found out. It will, for example, buy a dinner; and a dinner will keep a man

---

[3] See *Christianity and Liberalism*, 1923, pp. 142 f.

alive no matter how it is obtained. But just when I am buying the dinner for some poor man who needs it very badly indeed, an expert tells me that that useful result is being accomplished by a counterfeit note. "The miserable theorizer!," I may be tempted to exclaim, "the miserable traditionalist, the miserable demolisher of everything that pragmatism holds most dear! While he is discussing the question of the origin of that note— though every up-to-date man knows that the origin of a thing is unimportant, and that what is really important is the goal to which it tends—while he is going into learned details about the primitive history of that note, a poor man is suffering for lack of food." So it is, if the current view be correct, with faith; faith, we are told, is so very useful that we must not ask the question whether the things that it leads us to accept are true or false.

Plausible are the ways in which men are seeking to justify this circulation of counterfeit currency in the spiritual sphere; it is perfectly right, we are told, so long as it is not found out. That principle has even been ingeniously applied to the ordinary currency of the realm; if a counterfeit note were absolutely perfect, it has been said, so that by no possibility could it ever be detected, what harm should we be doing to a man if we passed it out to him with his change? Probably it will not be necessary to point out—at least to the readers of the present book—the fallacy in this moral *tour de force;* and that fallacy would really apply to the spiritual currency as well as to five-dollar notes. By circulating bad money we should be diminishing the value of good money, and so should be robbing the generality of our fellow-men. But after all, that question is purely academic; as a matter of fact counterfeit notes are never sure not to be found out. And neither is bad currency in the spiritual sphere. It is a dangerous thing to encourage faith in what is not true, for the sake of the immediate benefits which such faith brings; because the greater be the building that is erected on such a foundation, the greater will be the inevitable crash when the crash finally comes.

Such counterfeits should be removed, not in the interests of destruction, but in order to leave room for the pure gold the existence of which is implied by the presence of the counterfeits. There is counterfeit money in the world, but that does not mean that all money is counterfeit. Indeed it means the exact opposite. There could be no counterfeit money unless there were genuine money for it to imitate. And the principle applies to the spiritual realm. There is in the world much faith in what is false; but there could hardly be faith in what is false unless there were also somewhere faith in what is true. Now we Christians think that we have found faith in what is true when we have faith in the Lord Jesus Christ as He is offered to us in the gospel. We are well aware of what has been said against that gospel; we are well aware of the unpopularity that besets a man the moment he holds any one thing to be true and rejects as false whatever is contradictory to it; we are fully conscious of the risk that we are taking when we abandon a merely eclectic attitude and put all our confidence in one thing and one thing only. But we are ready to take the risk. This world is a dark place without Christ; we have found no other salvation either in ourselves or in others; and for our part, therefore, despite doubts and fears, we are prepared to take Christ at His word and launch forth into the deep at His command. It is a great venture, this venture of faith; there are difficulties in the way of it; we have not solved all mysteries or resolved all doubts. But though our minds are still darkened, though we have attained no rigidly mathematical proof, we have attained at least certitude enough to cause us to risk our lives. Will Christ desert us when we have thus committed ourselves to Him? There are men about us who tell us that He will; there are voices within us that whisper to us doubts; but we must act in accordance with the best light that is given us, and doing so we have decided for our part to distrust our doubts and base our lives, despite all, upon Christ.

The efficacy of faith, then, depends not upon the faith itself, considered as a psychological phenomenon, but upon the object of the faith, namely Christ. Faith is not regarded in the New Testament as itself a meritorious work or a meritorious condition of the soul; but it is regarded as a means which is used by the grace of God: the New Testament never says that a man is saved *on account of* his faith, but always that he is saved *through* his faith or *by means of* his faith; faith is merely the means which the Holy Spirit uses to apply to the individual soul the benefits of Christ's death.

And faith in one sense is a very simple thing. We have been engaged, indeed, in a sort of analysis of it;

but we have been doing so, not in the interests of complexity, but, on the contrary, in order to combat the
false notions by which simplicity is destroyed.   We
have not for a moment meant to imply that all the logical implications which we have found in faith are always consciously or separately in the mind of the man
who believes; mysterious indeed is the chemistry of the
soul, and a whole new world of thought as well as life
is often conveyed to a man in an experience of faith that
seems to be as simple as the falling of a leaf from the
bough and as inevitable as the flow of a mighty river
to the sea.   Certainly, at bottom, faith is in one sense
a very simple thing; it simply means that abandoning
the vain effort of earning one's way into God's presence
we accept the gift of salvation which Christ offers so
full and free.   Such is the "doctrine"—let us not be
afraid of the word—such is the "doctrine" of justification through faith alone.

That has been a liberating doctrine in the history of
the world; to it was due the breaking of mediaeval
bondage at the Reformation; to it is due ultimately the
civil liberty that we possess today.   And now that it
is being abandoned, civil liberty is slowly but steadily
being destroyed in the interests of a soul-killing collec-
tivism that is worse in some respects than the tyrannies
of the past.   Let us hope that the process may be arrested
in time.   If we are interested in what God thinks of
us, we shall not be deterred by what men think; the
very desire for justification in the sight of God makes us
independent of the judgment of men.   And if the very
desire for justification is liberating, how much more the

attainment of it!   The man who has been justified by
God, the man who has accepted as a free gift the condition of rightness with God which Christ offers, is not
a man who hopes that possibly, with due effort, if he
does not fail, he may finally win through to become a
child of God.   But he is a man who has already become a child of God.   If our being children of God depended in slightest measure upon us, we could never be
sure that we had attained the high estate.   But as a
matter of fact it does not depend upon us; it depends
only upon God.   It is not a reward that we have earned
but a gift that we have received.

CHAPTER VII

FAITH AND WORKS

Because of the fundamental nature of faith, as it has been set forth, on the basis of the New Testament teaching, in the last chapter, it is natural to find that in the New Testament faith, as the reception of a free gift, is placed in sharpest contrast with any intrusion of human merit; it is natural to find that faith is sharply contrasted with works. The contrast is really implied by the New Testament throughout, and in one book, the Epistle to the Galatians, it forms the express subject of the argument. That book from the beginning to the end is a mighty polemic in defence of the doctrine of justification by faith alone; and as such it has rightly been called the Magna Charta of Christian liberty. At the beginning of the sixteenth century the world was lying in darkness; but God then raised up a man who read this Epistle with his own eyes, and the Reformation was born. So it may be in our own day. Again the world is sinking into bondage; the liberty of the sons of God is again giving place to the bondage of a religion of merit: but God still lives, and His Spirit again may bring the charter of our liberty to light.

Meanwhile a strange darkness covers the eyes of men; the message of the great Epistle, so startlingly clear to the man whose eyes have been opened, is hidden by a mass of misinterpretation as absurd in its way as the mediaeval rubbish of the fourfold sense of Scripture which the Reformation brushed aside. Grammatico-historical interpretation is still being favored in theory, but despite is being done to it (by preachers if not by scholars) in practice; and the Apostle is being made to say anything that men wish him to have said. A new Reformation, we think, like the Reformation of the sixteenth century, would be marked, among other things, by a return to plain common sense; and the Apostle would be allowed, despite our likes and dislikes, to say what he really meant to say.

But what did the Apostle, in the Epistle to the Galatians, really mean to say; against what was he writing in that great polemic; and what was he setting up in place of that which he was endeavoring to destroy?

The answer which many modern writers are giving to this question is that the Apostle is arguing merely against an external ceremonial religion in the interests of a religion based on great principles; that he is arguing against a piecemeal conception of morality which makes morality consist in a series of disconnected rules, in the interests of a conception that draws out human conduct naturally from a central root in love; that he is arguing, in other words, against the "letter of the law" in the interests of its "spirit."

This interpretation, we think, involves an error which cuts away the very vitals of the Christian religion. Like other fatal errors, indeed, it does contain an element of truth; in one passage, at least, in the Epistle to the Galatians Paul does seem to point to the external character of the ceremonial law as being inferior to the higher (or to use modern terminology, more "spiritual") stage to which religion, under the new dispensation, had come. But that passage is isolated merely, and certainly does not in itself give the key to the meaning of the Epistle. On the contrary, even in that passage, when it is taken in its context, the inferiority of the old dispensation as involving ceremonial requirements is really put merely as a sign of an inferiority that is deeper still; and it is that deeper inferiority which the Epistle as a whole is concerned to set forth. The ceremonial character of the Old Testament law, so inferior to the inwardness of the new dispensation, was intended by God to mark the inferiority of any dispensation of law as distinguished from a dispensation of grace.

Of course a word of caution should again at this point be injected. Paul never means to say that the old dispensation was merely a dispensation of law; he always admits, and indeed insists upon, the element of grace which ran through it from beginning to end, the element of grace which appeared in the Promise. But his opponents in Galatia had rejected that element of grace; and their use of the Old Testament law, as distinguished from its right use as a schoolmaster unto Christ, really made of the old dispensation a dispensation of law and nothing more.

What then, according to Paul, was the real, underlying inferiority of that dispensation of law; how was it to be contrasted with the new dispensation which Christ had ushered in? It is hard to see how the answer to this question can really be regarded as obscure;

the Apostle has poured forth his very soul to make the matter plain. Most emphatically the contrast was not between a lower law and a higher law; it was not between an external, piecemeal conception of the law and a conception which reduces it to great underlying principles; but it was a contrast between any kind of law, no matter how sublimated, provided only it be conceived of as a way of obtaining merit, and the absolutely free grace of God.

This contrast is entirely missed by the interpretation that prevails popularly in the Modernist Church: the advocates of "salvation by character" have supposed that the polemic of the Apostle was turned merely against certain forgotten ceremonialists of long ago, while in reality it is turned quite as much against them. It is turned, indeed, against any man who seeks to stand in God's sight on the basis of his own merit instead of on the basis of the sacrifice which Christ offered to satisfy divine justice upon the cross. The truth is that the prevailing Modernist interpretation of Galatians, which is in some respects apparently just the interpretation favored by the Roman Church, makes the Apostle say almost the exact opposite of what he means.

The Modernist return to mediaevalism in the interpretation of Galatians is no isolated thing, but is only one aspect of a misinterpretation of the whole Bible; in particular it is closely akin to a misinterpretation of a great sentence in one of the other Epistles of Paul. The sentence to which we refer is found in II Corinthians iii. 6: "The letter killeth, but the Spirit giveth life."

That sentence is perhaps the most frequently misused utterance in the whole Bible. It has indeed in this respect much competition: many phrases in the New Testament are being used today to mean almost their exact opposite, as for example, when the words, "God in Christ" and the like, are made to be an expression of the vague pantheism so popular just now, or as when the entire gospel of redemption is regarded as a mere symbol of an optimistic view of man against which that doctrine was in reality a stupendous protest, or as when the doctrine of the incarnation is represented as indicating the essential oneness of God and man! One is reminded constantly at the present time of the way in which the Gnostics of the second century used Biblical texts to support their thoroughly un-Biblical systems. The historical method of study, in America at least, is very generally being abandoned; and the New Testament writers are being made to say almost anything that twentieth-century readers could have wished them to say.

This abandonment of scientific historical method in exegesis, which is merely one manifestation of the intellectual decadence of our day, appears at countless points in contemporary religious literature; but at no point does it appear with greater clearness than in connection with the great utterance in II Corinthians to which we have referred. The words: "The letter killeth, but the Spirit giveth life," are constantly interpreted to mean that we are perfectly justified in taking the law of God with a grain of salt; they are held to indicate that Paul was no "literalist," but a "Liberal," who believed that the Old Testament was not true in detail and the Old Testament law was not valid in detail, but that all God requires is that we should extract the few great principles which the Bible teaches and not insist upon the rest. In short, the words are held to involve a contrast between the letter of the law and "the spirit of the law"; they are held to mean that literalism is deadly, while attention to great principles keeps a man intellectually and spiritually alive.

Thus has one of the greatest utterances in the New Testament been reduced to comparative triviality—a triviality with a kernel of truth in it, to be sure, but triviality all the same. The triviality, indeed, is merely relative; no doubt it is important to observe that attention to the general sense of a book or a law is far better than such a reading of details as that the context in which the details are found is ignored. But all that is quite foreign to the meaning of the Apostle in this passage, and is, though quite true and quite important in its place, trivial in comparison with the tremendous thing that Paul is here endeavoring to say.

What Paul is really doing here is not contrasting the letter of the law with the spirit of the law, but contrasting the law of God with the Spirit of God. When he says, "The letter killeth," he is making no contemptuous reference to a pedantic literalism which shrivels the soul; but he is setting forth the terrible majesty of God's law. The letter, the "thing written," in the law of God, says Paul, pronounces a dread sen-

tence of death upon the transgressor; but the Holy
Spirit of God, as distinguished from the law, gives life.

The law of God, Paul means, is, as law, external.
It is God's holy will to which we must conform; but
it contains in itself no promise of its fulfilment; it is
one thing to have the law written, and quite another
thing to have it obeyed. In fact, because of the sinful-
ness of our hearts, because of the power of the flesh, the
recognition of God's law only makes sin take on the
definite form of transgression; it only makes sin more
exceeding sinful. The law of God was written on
tables of stone or on the rolls of the Old Testament
books, but it was quite a different thing to get it written
in the hearts and lives of the people. So it is today.
The text is of very wide application. The law of God,
however it comes to us, is "letter"; it is a "thing written," external to the hearts and lives of men. It is
written in the Old Testament; it is written in the Sermon on the Mount; it is written in Jesus' stupendous
command of love for God and one's neighbor; it is
written in whatever way we become conscious of the
commands of God. Let no one say that such an extension of the text involves that very anti-historical mod-
ernizing which we have just denounced; on the contrary
it is amply justified by Paul himself. "When the Gentiles," Paul says, "which have not the law, do by nature
the things contained in the law, these, having not the
law, are a law unto themselves."[1] The Old Testament
law is just a clear, authentic presentation of a law of
God under which all men stand.

---

[1] Rom. ii: 14.

And that law, according to Paul, issues a dreadful sentence of eternal death. "The soul that sinneth, it shall die"; not the hearer of the law is justified but the doer of it. And, alas, none are doers; all have sinned. The law of God is holy and just and good; it is inexorable; and we have fallen under its just condemnation.

That is at bottom what Paul means by the words, "The letter killeth." He does not mean that attention to pedantic details shrivels and deadens the soul. No doubt that is true, at least within certain limits; it is a useful thought. But it is trivial indeed compared with what Paul means. Something far more majestic, far more terrible, is meant by the Pauline phrase. The "letter" that the Apostle means is the same as the curse of God's law that he speaks of in Galatians; it is the dreadful handwriting of ordinances that was against us; and the death with which it kills is the eternal death of those who are forever separated from God.

But that is not all of the text. "The letter killeth," Paul says, "but the Spirit giveth life." There is no doubt about what he means by "the Spirit." He does not mean the "spirit of the law" as contrasted with the letter; he certainly does not mean the lax interpretation of God's commands which is dictated by human lust or pride; he certainly does not mean the spirit of man. No real student of Paul, whatever be his own religious views, can doubt, I think, but that the Apostle means the Spirit of God. God's law brings death because of sin; but God's Spirit, applying to the soul the redemption offered by Christ, brings life. The thing that is written killeth; but the Holy Spirit, in the new birth, or, as Paul says, the new creation, giveth life.

The contrast runs all through the New Testament. Hopelessness under the law is described, for example, in the seventh chapter of Romans. "Oh wretched man that I am! who shall deliver me from the body of this death?"[2]   But this hopelessness is transcended by the gospel. "For the law of the Spirit of life in Christ Jesus hath made me free from the law of sin and death."[3] The law's just sentence of condemnation was borne for us by Christ who suffered in our stead; the handwriting of ordinances which was against us—the dreadful "letter"— was nailed to the cross, and we have a fresh start in the full favor of God.   And in addition to this new and right relation to God, the Spirit of God also gives the sinner a new birth and makes him a new creature. The New Testament from beginning to end deals gloriously with this work of grace.   The giving of life of which Paul speaks in this text is the new birth, the new creation; it is Christ who liveth in us.   Here is the fulfillment of the great prophecy of Jeremiah: "But this shall be the covenant that I will make with the house of Israel; After those days, saith the Lord, I will put my law in their inward parts, and write it in their hearts."[4] The law is no longer for the Christian a command which it is for him by his own strength to obey, but its requirements are fulfilled through the mighty power of the Holy Spirit.   There is the glorious free-

[2] Rom. vii: 24.

[3] Rom. viii: 2.

[4] Jer. xxxi: 33.

dom of the gospel. The gospel does not abrogate God's law, but it makes men love it with all their hearts.

How is it with us? The law of God stands over us; we have offended against it in thought, word and deed; its majestic "letter" pronounces a sentence of death against our sin. Shall we obtain a specious security by ignoring God's law, and by taking refuge in an easier law of our own devising? Or shall the Lord Jesus, as He is offered to us in the gospel, wipe out the sentence of condemnation that was against us, and shall the Holy Spirit write God's law in our heart, and make us doers of the law and not hearers only? So and only so will the great text be applied to us: "The letter killeth, but the Spirit giveth life."

The alternative that underlies this verse, then, and that becomes explicit in Galatians also, is not an alternative between an external or ceremonial religion and what men would now call (by a misuse of the New Testament word) a "spiritual" religion, important though that alternative no doubt is; but it is an alternative between a religion of merit and a religion of grace. The Epistle to the Galatians is directed just as much against the modern notion of "salvation by character" or salvation by "making Christ Master" in the life or salvation by a mere attempt to put into practice "the principles of Jesus," as it is directed against the Jewish ceremonialists of long ago: for what the Apostle is concerned to deny is any intrusion of human merit into the work by which salvation is obtained. That work, according to the Epistle to the Galatians and according to the whole New Testament, is the work of God and of God alone.

At this point appears the full poignancy of the great Epistle with which we have been dealing. Paul is not merely arguing that a man is justified by faith—so much no doubt his opponents, the Judaizers, admitted—but he is arguing that a man is justified by faith *alone*. What the Judaizers said was not that a man is justified by works, but that he is justified by faith *and* works —exactly the thing that is being taught by the Roman Catholic Church today. No doubt they admitted that it was necessary for a man to have faith in Christ in order to be saved; but they held that it was also necessary for him to keep the law the best he could; salvation, according to them, was not by faith alone and not by works alone but by faith and works together. A man's obedience to the law of God, they held, was not, indeed, sufficient for salvation, but it was necessary; and it became sufficient when it was supplemented by Christ.

Against this compromising solution of the problem, the Apostle insists upon a sharp alternative: a man may be saved by works (if he keeps the law perfectly), or he may be saved by faith; but he cannot possibly be saved by faith and works together. Christ, according to Paul, will do everything or nothing; if righteousness is in slightest measure obtained by our obedience to the law, then Christ died in vain; if we trust in slightest measure in our own good works, then we have turned away from grace and Christ profiteth us nothing.

To the world, that may seem to be a hard saying; but it is not a hard saying to the man who has ever

been at the foot of the Cross; it is not a hard saying to
the man who has first known the bondage of the law,
the weary effort at establishment of his own righteousness in the presence of God, and then has come to understand, as in a wondrous flash of light, that Christ has
done all, and that the weary bondage was vain. What a
great theologian is the Christian heart—the Christian
heart that has been touched by redeeming grace! The
man who has felt the burden of sin roll away at the
sight of the Cross, who has said of the Lord Jesus, "He
loved me and gave Himself for me," who has sung with
Toplady: "Nothing in my hand I bring, Simply to
Thy cross I cling"—that man knows in his heart of
hearts that the Apostle is right, that to trust Christ only
for part is not to trust Him at all, that our own righteousness is insufficient even to bridge the smallest gap
which might be left open between us and God, that
there is no hope unless we can safely say to the Lord
Jesus, without shadow of reservation, without shadow
of self-trust: "Thou must save, and Thou alone."

That is the centre of the Christian religion—the absolutely undeserved and sovereign grace of God, saving
sinful men by the gift of Christ upon the cross. Condemnation comes by merit; salvation comes only by
grace; condemnation is earned by man; salvation is
given by God. The fact of the grace of God runs
through the New Testament like a golden thread; indeed for it the New Testament exists. It is found in
the words which Jesus spoke in the days of His flesh,
as in the parables of the servant coming in from the
field and of the laborers in the vineyard; it is found

more fully set forth after the redeeming work was done, after the Lord had uttered his triumphant "It is finished" upon the cross. Everywhere the basis of the New Testament is the same—the mysterious, incalculable, wondrous, grace of God. "The wages of sin is death; but the gift of God is eternal life through Jesus Christ our Lord."[5]

The reception of that gift is faith: faith means not doing something but receiving something; it means not the earning of a reward but the acceptance of a gift. A man can never be said to obtain a thing for himself if he obtains it by faith; indeed to say that he obtains it by faith is only another way of saying that he does not obtain it for himself but permits another to obtain it for him. Faith, in other words, is not active but passive; and to say that we are saved by faith is to say that we do not save ourselves but are saved only by the one in whom our faith is reposed; the faith of man presupposes the sovereign grace of God.

Even yet, however, we have not sounded the full depths of the New Testament teaching; we have not yet fully set forth the place in salvation which the Bible assigns to the grace of God. A sort of refuge, in what we have said so far, may seem to have been left for the pride of man. Man does not save himself, we have said; God saves him. But man accepts that salvation by faith; and faith, though a negative act, seems to be a kind of act: salvation is freely offered by God; the offer of it does not depend at all upon man; yet a man

---

[5] Rom. vi: 23.

might seem to obtain a sort of merit by not resisting that offer when once it is given him by God.

But even this last refuge of human pride is searched out and destroyed by the teaching of God's Word; for the Bible represents even faith itself—little merit as it could in any case involve—as the work of the Spirit of God. The Spirit, according to a true summary of the New Testament, works faith in us and thereby unites us to Christ in our effectual calling; sovereign and resistless is God's grace; and our faith is merely the means which the Spirit uses to apply to us the benefits of Christ's redeeming work.

The means was of God's choosing, not ours; and it is not for us to say, "What doest Thou?" Yet even we, weak and ignorant though we are, can see, I think, why this particular means was chosen to unite us to Christ; why faith was chosen instead of love, for example, as the channel by which salvation could enter into our lives. Love is active; faith is passive; hence faith not love was chosen. If the Bible had said that we are saved by love, then even though our love was altogether the gift of the Spirit, we might have thought that it was our own, and so we might have claimed salvation as our right. But as it is, not only were we saved by grace, but because of the peculiar means which God used to save us, we *knew* that we were saved by grace; it was of the very nature of faith to make us know that we were not saving ourselves. Even before we could love as we ought to love, even before we could do anything or feel anything aright, we were saved by faith; we were saved by abandoning all confidence in our own thoughts or feelings or actions and by simply allowing ourselves to be saved by God.

In one sense, indeed, we were saved by love; that indeed is an even profounder fact than that we were saved by faith. Yes, we were saved by love, but it was by a greater love than the love in our cold and sinful hearts; we were saved by love, but it was not our love for God but God's love for us, God's love for us by which he gave the Lord Jesus to die for us upon the cross. "Herein is love, not that we loved God, but that He loved us, and sent his Son to be the propitiation for our sins."[6] That love alone is the love that saves. And the means by which it saves is faith.

Thus the beginning of the Christian life is not an achievement but an experience; the soul of the man who is saved is not, at the moment of salvation, active, but passive; salvation is the work of God and God alone. That does not mean that the Christian is unconscious when salvation enters his life; it does not mean that he is placed in a trance, or that his ordinary faculties are in abeyance; on the contrary the great transition often seems to be a very simple thing; overpowering emotional stress is by no means always present; and faith is always a conscious condition of the soul. There is, moreover, a volitional aspect of faith, in which it appears to the man who believes to be induced by a conscious effort of his will, a conscious effort of his will by which he resolves to cease trying to save himself and resolves to accept, instead, the salvation offered by Christ. The preacher of the gospel ought to appeal, we think, in

---

[6] I John iv: 10.

every way in his power, to the conscious life of the man
whom he is trying to win; he ought to remove intellectual objections against the truth of Christianity, and
adduce positive arguments; he ought to appeal to the
emotions; he ought to seek, by exhortation, to move the
will. All these means may be used, and have been used
countless times, by the Spirit of God; and certainly we
have not intended to disparage them by anything that
we have just said. But what we do maintain is that
though necessary they are not sufficient; they will never
bring a man to faith in Christ unless there is with them
the mysterious, regenerating power of the Spirit of God.
We are not presuming to treat here the psychology of
faith; and certainly we do not think that such a psychology of faith is at all necessary to the man who believes; indeed the less he thinks about his own states of
consciousness and the more he thinks about Christ the
better it will often be for his soul. But this much at
least can be said: even conscious states can be induced
in supernatural fashion by the Spirit of God, and such
a conscious state is the faith by which a man first accepts Christ as his Saviour from sin.

But if the beginning of the Christian life is thus not
an achievement but an experience, if a man is not really
active, but passive, when he is saved, if faith is to be
placed in sharp contrast with works, what becomes of
the ethical character of the Christian religion, what becomes of the stimulus which it has always given to
human individuality and to the sense of human worth,
what becomes of the vigorous activity which, in marked
contrast with some of the other great religions of the

world, it has always encouraged in its adherents? Such
questions are perfectly legitimate; and they show that
we are very far from having given, up to the present
point, any adequate account of the relation, in the
Christian religion, between faith and works, or between
doctrine and life.

That relation must therefore now be examined,
though still briefly, a little more in detail.

The examination may best be begun by a consideration of what has been regarded by some devout readers
of the Bible as a serious difficulty, namely the apparent
contradiction between the second chapter of Galatians
and the second chapter of the Epistle of James. "A
man is not justified by the works of the law, but only
through faith in Christ Jesus," says Paul;[7] "Ye see then
how that by works a man is justified and not by faith
only," says James.[8] These two verses in their juxta-
position constitute an ancient Biblical difficulty. In the
verse from Galatians a man is said to become right with
God by faith alone apart from works; in the verse from
James he is said to become right with God not by faith
alone but by faith and works. If the verses are taken
out of their wider context and placed side by side, a
contradiction could scarcely seem to be more complete.

The Pauline doctrine of justification by faith alone,
which we have just treated at considerable length, is,
as we have seen, the very foundation of Christian liberty. It makes our standing with God dependent not

[7] Gal. ii: 16. It is evident from the immediate context that
this is the correct translation.

[8] James ii: 24.

at all upon what we have done, but altogether upon what God has done. If our salvation depended upon what we had done, then, according to Paul, we should still be bondslaves; we should still be endeavoring feverishly to keep God's law so well that at the end we might possibly win His favor. It would be a hopeless endeavor because of the deadly guilt of sin; we should be like debtors endeavoring to pay, but in the very effort getting deeper and deeper into debt. But as it is, in accordance with the gospel, God has granted us His favor as an absolutely free gift; He has brought us into right relation to Himself not on the basis of any merit of ours, but altogether on the basis of the merit of Christ. Great is the guilt of our sins; but Christ took it all upon Himself when He died for us on Calvary. We do not need, then, to make ourselves good before we become God's children; but we can come to God just as we are, all laden with our sins, and be quite certain that the guilt of sin will be removed and that we shall be received. When God looks upon us, to receive us or to cast us off, it is not we that He regards but our great Advocate, Christ Jesus the Lord.

Such is the glorious certainty of the gospel. The salvation of the Christian is certain because it depends altogether upon God; if it depended in slightest measure upon us, the certainty of it would be gone. Hence appears the vital importance of the great Reformation doctrine of justification by faith alone; that doctrine is at the very centre of Christianity. It means that acceptance with God is not something that we earn; it is not something that is subject to the wretched uncertainties of human endeavor; but it is a free gift of God. It may seem strange that we should be received by the holy God as His children; but God has chosen to receive us; it has been done on His responsibility not ours; He has a right to receive whom He will into His presence; and in the mystery of His grace He has chosen to receive us.

That central doctrine of the Christian faith is really presupposed in the whole New Testament; but it is made particularly plain in the Epistles of Paul. It is such passages as the eighth chapter of Romans, the second and third chapters of Galatians, and the fifth chapter of II Corinthians, which set forth in plainest fashion the very centre of the gospel.

But in the Epistle of James there seems at first sight to be a discordant note in this great New Testament chorus. "Ye see then," says James, "how that by works a man is justified, and not by faith only." If that means that a man is pronounced righteous before God partly because of the merit of his own works and only partly because of the sacrifice of Christ accepted by faith, then James holds exactly the position of the bitter opponents of Paul who are combated in the Epistle to the Galatians. Those opponents, the "Judaizers" as they are called, held, as we have seen, that faith in Christ is necessary to salvation (in that they agreed with Paul), but they held that the merit of one's own observance of the law of God is also necessary. A man is saved, not by faith alone and not by works alone, but by faith and works together—that was apparently the formula of the Judaizing opponents of Paul. The

Apostle rightly saw that that formula meant a return to bondage. If Christ saves us only part way, and leaves a gap to be filled up by our own good works, then we can never be certain that we are saved. The awakened conscience sees clearly that our own obedience to God's law is not the kind of obedience that is really required; it is not that purity of the heart which is demanded by the teaching and example of our Lord. Our obedience to the law is insufficient to bridge even the smallest gap; we are unprofitable servants, and if we ever enter into an account with our Judge we are undone. Christ has done nothing for us or He has done everything; to depend even in smallest measure upon our own merit is the very essence of unbelief; we must trust Christ for nothing or we must trust Him for all. Such is the teaching of the Epistle to the Galatians.

But in the Epistle of James we seem at first sight to be in a different circle of ideas. "Justified by faith alone," says Paul; "Justified not by faith alone," says James. It has been a difficulty to many readers of the Bible. But like other apparent contradictions in the Bible it proves to be a contradiction merely of form and not of content; and it serves only to lead the devout reader into a deeper and fuller understanding of the truth.

The solution of the difficulty appears in the definition of the word "faith." The apparent contradiction is due simply to the fact that when James in this chapter says that "faith" alone is insufficient, he means a different thing by the word "faith" from that which Paul means by it when he says that faith is all-sufficient.

The kind of faith which James is pronouncing insufficient is made clear in the nineteenth verse of the same
chapter: "Thou believest that there is one God; thou
doest well: the devils also believe, and tremble." The
kind of faith which James pronounces insufficient is
the faith which the devils also have; it is a mere intellectual apprehension of the facts about God or Christ,
and it involves no acceptance of those facts as a gift
of God to one's own soul. But it is not that kind of
faith which Paul means when he says that a man is
saved by faith alone. Faith is indeed intellectual; it
involves an apprehension of certain things as facts; and
vain is the modern effort to divorce faith from knowledge. But although faith is intellectual, it is not only
intellectual. You cannot have faith without having
knowledge; but you will not have faith if you have
only knowledge. Faith is the acceptance of a gift at
the hands of Christ. We cannot accept the gift without
knowing certain things about the gift and about the
giver. But we might know all those things and still
not accept the gift. We might know what the gift is
and still not accept it. Knowledge is thus absolutely
necessary to faith, but it is not all that is necessary.
Christ comes offering us that right relation to God
which He wrought for us on the cross. Shall we accept the gift or shall we hold it in disdain? The acceptance of the gift is called faith. It is a very wonderful thing; it involves a change of the whole nature of
man; it involves a new hatred of sin and a new hunger
and thirst after righteousness. Such a wonderful change
is not the work of man; faith itself is given us by the

Spirit of God. Christians never make themselves Christians; but they are made Christians by God.

All that is clear from what has already been said. But it is quite inconceivable that a man should be given this faith in Christ, that he should accept this gift which Christ offers, and still go on contentedly in sin. For the very thing which Christ offers us is salvation from sin—not only salvation from the guilt of sin, but also salvation from the power of sin. The very first thing that the Christian does, therefore, is to keep the law of God: he keeps it no longer as a way of earning his salvation—for salvation has been given him freely by God—but he keeps it joyously as a central part of salvation itself. The faith of which Paul speaks is, as Paul himself says, a faith that works through love; and love is the fulfilling of the whole law. Paul would have agreed fully with James that the faith of which James speaks in our passage is quite insufficient for salvation. The faith that Paul means when he speaks of justification by faith alone is a faith that works.

But if the faith regarded insufficient by James is different from the faith commended by Paul, so also the works commended by James are different from the works regarded inefficacious by Paul. Paul is speaking of works *of the law,* he is speaking of works that are intended to acquire merit in order that God's favor may be earned; James on the other hand is speaking of works like Abraham's sacrifice of Isaac that are the result of faith and show that faith is real faith.

The difference, then, between Paul and James is a difference of terminology, not of meaning. That difference of terminology shows that the Epistle of James was written at a very early time, before the controversy with the Judaizers had arisen and before the terminology had become fixed. If James had been writing after the terminology had become fixed, what he would have said is that although a man is justified by faith alone and not at all by works, yet one must be sure that the faith is real faith and not a mere intellectual assent like that of the demons who believe and tremble. What he actually does is to say just that in different words. James is not correcting Paul, then; he is not even correcting a misinterpretation of Paul; but he is unconsciously preparing for Paul; he is preparing well for the clearer and more glorious teaching of the great Epistles.

The Epistle of James ought to be given its due place in the nurture of the Christian life. It has sometimes been regarded as the Epistle of works. But that does not mean that this Epistle ignores the deeper and more meditative elements in the Christian life. James is no advocate of a mere "gospel of street-cleaning"; he is no advocate of what is falsely called today a "practical," as distinguished from a doctrinal, Christianity; he is not a man who seeks to drown an inward disquiet by a bustling philanthropy. On the contrary he is a great believer in the power of prayer; he exalts faith and denounces doubt; he humbles man and glorifies God: "Go to now, ye that say, To day or to morrow we will go into such a city, and continue there a year, and buy and sell, and get gain; whereas ye know not what shall be on the morrow. For what is your life? It is even a vapour, that appeareth for a little time, and then vanisheth away. For that ye ought to say, If the Lord will, we shall live, and do this, or that."[9] The man who wrote these words was no mere advocate of a "practical" religion of this world; he was no mere advocate of what is called today "the social gospel"; but he was a man who viewed this world, as the whole New Testament views it, in the light of eternity.

So the lesson of James may be learned without violence being done to the deepest things of the Christian faith—certainly without violence being done to the gospel which Paul proclaims. It was as clear to Paul as it was to James that men who had been saved by faith could not continue to live unholy lives. "Be not deceived," says Paul: "neither fornicators, nor idolaters, nor adulterers . . . . nor thieves, nor covetous, nor drunkards, nor revilers, nor extortioners, shall inherit the kingdom of God."[10] It is difficult to see how anything could be much plainer than that. Paul just as earnestly as James insists upon the ethical or practical character of Christianity; Paul as well as James insists upon purity and unselfishness in conduct as an absolutely necessary mark of the Christian life. A Christian, according to Paul (as also really according to James), is saved not by himself but by God; but he is saved by God not in order that he may continue in sin,

[9] James iv: 13 f.
[10] I Cor. vi: 9 f.

but in order that he may conquer sin and attain unto holiness.

Indeed so earnest is Paul about this matter that at times it looks almost as though he believed Christians even in this life to be altogether sinless, as though he believed that if they were not sinless they were not Christians at all. Such an interpretation of the Epistles would indeed be incorrect; it is contradicted, in particular, by the loving care with which the Apostle exhorted and encouraged those members of his congregations who had been overtaken in a fault. As a pastor of souls Paul recognized the presence of sin even in those who were within the household of faith; and dealt with it not only with severity but also with patience and love. Nevertheless the fact is profoundly significant that in the great doctrinal passages of the Epistles Paul makes very little reference (though such reference is not altogether absent) to the presence of sin in Christian men. How is that fact to be explained? I think it is to be explained by the profound conviction of the Apostle that although sin is actually found in Christians it does not belong there; it is never to be acquiesced in for one single moment, but is to be treated as a terrible anomaly that simply ought not to be.

Thus according to Paul the beginning of the new life is followed by a battle a battle against sin. In that battle, as is not the case with the beginning of it, the Christian does co-operate with God; he is helped by God's Spirit, but he himself, and not only God's Spirit in him, is active in the fight.

At the beginning of the Christian life there is an act

of God and of God alone. It is called in the New Testament the new birth or (as Paul calls it) the new creation. In that act no part whatever is contributed by the man who is born again. And no wonder! A man who is dead—either dead in physical death or "dead in trespasses and sins"—can do nothing whatever, at least in the sphere in which he is dead. If he could do anything in that sphere, he would not be dead. Such a man who is dead in trespasses and sins is raised to new life in the new birth or the new creation. To that new birth he himself cannot contribute at all, any more than he contributed to his physical birth. But birth is followed by life; and though a man is not active in his birth he is active in the life that follows. So it is also in the spiritual realm. We did not contribute at all to our new birth; that was an act of God alone. But that new birth is followed by a new life, and in the new life we have been given by Him who begat us anew the power of action; it is that power of action that is involved in birth. Thus the Christian life is begun by an act of God alone; but it is continued by co-operation between God and man. The possibility of such co-operation is due indeed only to God; it has not been achieved in slightest measure by us; it is the supreme wonder of God's grace. But once given by God it is not withdrawn.

Thus the Christian life in this world is not passive but active; it consists in a mighty battle against sin. That battle is a winning battle, because the man that engages in it has been made alive in the first place by God, and because he has a great Companion to help him in every turn of the fight. But, though a winning battle, it is a battle all the same; and it is not only God's battle but ours. The faith of which we have been speaking consists not in doing something but in receiving something; but it is followed every time by a life in which great things are done.

This aspect of faith is put in classic fashion by the Apostle Paul in a wonderful phrase in the Epistle to the Galatians. "Neither circumcision availeth any thing," says Paul, "nor uncircumcision; but faith which worketh by love."[11] In that phrase, "faith which worketh by love," or, more literally, "faith working through love," a whole world of experience is compressed within the compass of four words.

Surely that is a text for a practical age; the world may perhaps again become interested in faith if it sees that faith is a thing that works. And certainly our practical age cannot afford to reject assistance wherever it can be found; for the truth is that this practical age seems just now to be signally failing to accomplish results even on its own ground; it seems to be signally failing to "make things go."

Strangely enough the present failure of the world to make things go is due just to that emphasis upon efficiency which might seem to make failure impossible; it is the paradox of efficiency that it can be attained only by those who do not make it the express object of their desires. The modern one-sided emphasis upon the practical has hindered the progress of humanity, we think, in at least two ways.

---

[11] Gal. v: 6.

The first way has already been treated in what precedes. Men are so eager about the work, we observed, that they have neglected a proper choice of means to accomplish it; they think that they can make use of religion, as a means to an end, without settling the question of the truth of any particular religion; they think that they can make use of faith as a beneficent psychological phenomenon without determining whether the thing that is believed is true or false. The whole effort, as we observed, is vain; such a pragmatist use of faith really destroys the thing that is being used. If therefore the work is to proceed, we cannot in this pragmatist fashion avoid, but must first face and settle, the question of the means.

In the second place, men are so eager today about the work that they are sometimes indifferent to the question what particular kind of work it shall be. The efficient, energetic man is often being admired by the world at large, and particularly by himself, quite irrespective of the character of his achievements. It often seems to make little difference whether a man engages in the accumulation of material wealth or in the quest of political power or in the management of schools and hospitals and charities. Whether he engages in robbery or in missions, he is sure of recognition, provided only he succeeds, provided only he is "a man who does things." But however stimulating such a prizing of work for its own sake may be to the individual, it is obviously not conducive to any great advance for humanity as a whole. If my labor is going to be opposed to the work of my neighbor, we might both of us enjoy a good, old-fashioned, comfortable rest, so far as any general progress is concerned. Our efforts simply cancel each other. Consequently, although a great deal of energy is being displayed in the world today, one cannot help having the feeling that a vast deal of it is being wasted. The truth is that if we are to be truly practical men, we must first be theorizers. We must first settle upon some one great task and some one great force for its accomplishment.

The Pauline text makes proposals in both directions. It proposes both a task and a force to accomplish it. "Faith working itself out through love"—love is the work, faith the means.

It should be noticed in the first place that this work and this means are open to everyone. In Christ Jesus neither circumcision availeth anything nor uncircumcision; there is neither Jew nor Greek, there is neither bond nor free, there is no male and female; nothing is required except what is common to all men. If we like the work we cannot say that it is beyond our reach.

The work is love, and what that is Paul explains in the last division of the same Epistle. It is not a mere emotion, it is not even a mere benevolent desire, it is a practical thing. We sometimes say of a rather unprincipled and dissipated man: "He is weak, but he has a good heart." Such mere good-heartedness is not Christian love. Christian love includes not merely the wish for the welfare of one's fellow-men, not merely even the willingness to help, but also the power. In order to love in the Christian sense, a man must be not only benevolent, but also strong and good; he must love his fellow-men enough to build up his own strength in order to use it for their benefit.

Such a task is very different from much of the work that is actually being done in the world. In the first place, it is a spiritual not a material work. It is really astonishing how many men are almost wholly absorbed in purely material things. Very many men seem to have no higher conception of work than that of making the dirt fly: the greatest nation is thought to be the nation that has the largest income and the biggest battleships; the greatest university, even, to be the one that has the finest laboratories. Such practical materialism need not be altogether selfish; the production of material goods may be desired for others as well as for one's self. Socialism may be taken as an example. It is not altogether selfish. But—at least in its most consistent forms—it errs in supposing that the proper distribution of material wealth will be a panacea. Indeed, such a habit of thought has not been altogether absent from the Church itself. Wherever the notion is cherished that the relief of physical suffering is somehow more important—more practical—than the welfare of the human spirit, there material things are being made the chief object of pursuit. And that is not Christian love. Christian love does not, indeed, neglect men's physical welfare; it does not give a man a sermon when he needs bread. It relieves distress; it delights in affording even the simplest pleasure to a child. But it always does these things with the consciousness of the one inestimable gift that it has in reserve.

In the second place, Christian love is not merely

intellectual or emotional, but also moral. It involves
nothing less than the keeping of the whole moral law.
"For all the law is fulfilled in one word, even in this;
Thou shalt love thy neighbor as thyself."[12]   Christianity may provide a satisfactory world-view, it may
give men comfort and happiness, it may deprive death
of its terrors, it may produce the exaltation of religious
emotion; but it is not Christianity unless it makes men
better. Furthermore, love is a peculiar kind of observance of the moral law. It is not a mere performance of
a set of external acts. That may be hypocrisy or expediency. Nor is it a mere devotion to duty for duty's
sake. That is admirable and praiseworthy, but it is
the childhood stage of morality. The Christian is no
longer under the schoolmaster; his performance of the
law springs not from obedience to a stern voice of duty
but from an overpowering impulse; he *loves* the law
of the Lord; he does right because he cannot help it.

In the third place, love involves, I think, a peculiar
conception of the content of the law. It regards morality primarily as unselfishness. And what a vast deal
of the culture of the world, with all its pomp and
glitter, is selfish to the core! Genius exploits the plain
men; Christ died for them; and His disciples must
follow in the footsteps of their Lord.

In the fourth place, Christian love is not merely love
for man; it is also, and even primarily, love for God.
We have observed that love for God is not the means
by which we are saved: the New Testament does not
say "Thy love hath saved thee," but "Thy faith hath

---

[12] Gal. v: 14.

saved thee"; it does not say, "Love the Lord Jesus Christ, and thou shalt be saved," but "Believe on the Lord Jesus Christ, and thou shalt be saved." But that does not mean that the New Testament depreciates love; it does not mean that if a man did love, and always had loved, God the Father and the Lord Jesus Christ and his fellow-men, as he ought to love them, he would not be a saved man; it only means that because of sin no unregenerate man who has ever lived has actually done that. Love, according to the New Testament, is not the means of salvation, but it is the finest fruit of it; a man is saved by faith, not by love; but he is saved by faith in order that he may love.

Such, then, is the work. How may it be accomplished? "Simply by accomplishing it," says the "practical" man; "no appeal need be made except to the sovereign will; any time a man desires to stop his evil ways and begin to serve God and his fellow-men, the way is perfectly open for him to do it." Yet here is the remarkable thing: the way is always perfectly open, and yet the man never enters upon it; he always can, but never does. Some of us feel the logical necessity of seeking a common cause for such a uniform effect. And the common cause that we find is sin.

Of course if there is no such thing as sin, then nothing is needed to overcome it, and nothing stands in the way of Christian love. The existence of sin, as we observed, is quite generally denied in the modern world. It is denied in at least two ways. In the first place, men sometimes say in effect that there is no sin, but only imperfection; what we call "sin" is just one form of imperfection. If so, it may perhaps well be argued that the human will is sufficient for human tasks. We have obviously made at least some progress, it is said; we have advanced beyond the "stone age"; a continuation of the same efforts will no doubt bring us still further on our way; and as for perfection—that is as impossible for us in the very nature of things as infinity. In the second place, it is said, there is no sin but only sins. It is admitted that moral evil is different in kind from imperfection, but it is thought to possess no unity; every individual choice is thought to be independent of every other; a man is thought to be free every time to choose either good or evil; no one else can help him, it is said, and no one need help him.

Paul's view of sin is opposed to both of these. In the first place, sin, according to Paul, is deadly guilt, and in the second place it is not inherent merely in the individual acts. It is a mighty power, in the presence of which man is helpless. "It is no more I that do it, but sin that dwelleth in me."[13] "But," it may be objected, "what a dangerous form of expression that is! If it is no more I that do it, my responsibility is gone; how can I still feel guilt? If I am to be guilty, then sin must be a property simply and solely of my conscious acts." Yet experience curiously reverses such a priori reasoning; history teaches that the men who have actually felt most deeply the guilt of sin have been just the men who regarded it as a great force lying far beneath the individual acts. And a closer examination reveals the reason. If each act stands by itself, then a wrong choice at any par-

---

[13] Rom. vii: 17.

ticular time is, comparatively speaking, a trifling thing; it may easily be rectified next time. Such a philosophy can hardly produce any great horror and dread of sin. But if sin is regarded as a unitary power, irreconcilably opposed to what is good, then acts of sin, apparently trifling in themselves, show that we are under the dominion of such a power; the single wrong action can no longer be regarded by itself, but involves assent to a Satanic power, which then leads logically, irresistibly to the destruction of every right feeling, of every movement of love, of pity, of sympathy. When we come to see that what Paul calls the flesh is a mighty power, which is dragging us resistlessly down into an abyss of evil that has no bottom, then we feel our guilt and misery, then we look about for something stronger to help us than our own weak will.

Such a power is found by the Apostle Paul in faith; it is faith, he says, that produces, or works itself out in, the life of love. But what does Paul mean when he says that "faith works"? Certainly he does not mean what the modern pragmatist skeptic means when he uses the same words; certainly he does not mean that it is merely faith, considered as a psychological phenomenon, and independent of the truth or falsehood of its object, that does the work. What he does mean[14] is made abundantly clear in the last section of this same Epistle to the Galatians, where the life of love is presented in some detail. In that section nothing whatever is said about faith; it is not faith that is there represented as producing the life of love but the Spirit of God; the

[14] Compare *Christianity and Liberalism*, 1923, pp. 146 ff.

Spirit is there represented as doing exactly what, in the phrase "faith working through love," is ascribed to faith. The apparent contradiction leads us on to the right conception of faith. True faith, strictly speaking, does not do anything; it does not give, but receives. So when one says that we do something by faith that is just another way of saying that we do nothing—at least that we do nothing of ourselves. It is of the very nature of faith, strictly speaking, to do nothing. So when it is said that faith works through love, that means that through faith, instead of doing something for ourselves we allow some one else to help us. That force which enters our life at the beginning through faith, before we could do anything at all to please God, and which then strengthens and supports us in the battle that it has enabled us to begin, is the power of the Spirit of God.

So in the midst of a practical world, the Christian exhibits a practical life of love—a busy life of helpfulness, feeding the hungry, giving drink to the thirsty, receiving the strangers, clothing the naked, visiting the sick and the prisoners. And all that accomplished not by his own unaided efforts, not even merely by his own faith, but by the great object of his faith, the all-powerful God.

The Christian preacher, then, comes before the world with a great alternative. Shall we continue to depend upon our own efforts, or shall we receive by faith the power of God? Shall we content ourselves with the materials which this world affords, seeking by endlessly new combinations to produce a building that shall endure; or shall we build with the materials that have no flaw? Shall we give men new motives, or ask God to give them a new power? Shall we improve the world, or pray God to create a new world? The former alternatives have been tried and found wanting: the best of architects can produce no enduring building when all the materials are faulty; good motives are powerless when the heart is evil. Struggle as we may, we remain just a part of this evil world until, by faith, we cry: "Not by might, nor by power, but by Thy Spirit, O Lord of Hosts."

CHAPTER VIII

FAITH AND HOPE

It has been shown in the last chapter that the Christian life is a life of love, and that it is produced by the power of the Spirit of God received through faith in Christ. Such is the Christian work, and such is the power that accomplishes it. But what is the goal, what is the end for which the work is done?

That there is some goal beyond is suggested even by the very character of the means by which we accomplish even this present task. Just as the power of sin was not exhausted by the evil actions committed here and now, so the power of the Spirit is not exhausted by His present fruits. Just as sin was felt to contain infinite possibilities of evil, to be leading toward dreadful unfathomed depths, to contain a certain fearful looking for of judgment, so the power of the Spirit is felt to extend even beyond what He is now accomplishing. The Christian has within him a mysterious power of goodness, which is leading him by paths he knows not to an unknown and blessed country. The "practical" man of the world sees but little of the true life of the Christian. He sees but the bare outward manifestation of the infinite power within. It is no proof of the absolute truth of Christianity that it has made the world better; for that achievement it shares perhaps with other religions, though no doubt they have it

in far less degree. Other religions make men better:
but Christianity alone makes them good; for Christianity alone can exhibit one absolutely good human
life, and with it the promise that other lives will one
day be conformed to that. The Christian alone has
really close and vital contact with absolute goodness—
a goodness that contains in its very nature and presence
the promise that every last vestige of evil will finally
be removed.

So the Christian's love for his fellow men, which is
so much admired by the world, seems to the Christian
himself to be in one sense but a by-product; it is but
an effect of the greater love for God and but one step
in its unfolding. The relation of the Christian to that
force that sustains and guides him is not that of a dead
instrument in the hand of the workman, but that of a
free man to his loving father. The work is felt to be
all the more our work because it is also God's work.
That personal relation of love between the Christian
and his God is not seen by the world, but to the Christian it, and it alone, contains the promise of final goodness.

The Christian, then, produces the practical life of
love on the way to something greater; the Christian
lives by hope. That is sometimes made a reproach.
The Christian does what is right, it is said, because of
the rewards of heaven. How much nobler is the man
who does what is right simply because it is right, or
because it will lead to the happiness of generations yet
unborn, even though he believes that for himself the
grave ends all! The reproach would perhaps be justi-

fied if heaven involves mere selfish enjoyment. But as a matter of fact heaven involves not merely enjoyment, not merely happiness, but also goodness, and goodness realized in communion with the One who alone is good. To regard that communion as broken off forever in death does not in actual practice lead, as at first sight it might seem as though it would naturally lead, to a height of unselfish service in which without thought of individual survival a man would live for the sake of the race. For the race is worthy of a man's service, not if it is composed of mere creatures of a day, whose life is essentially like the life of the beasts, but only if it is composed of men with immortal souls. A degraded view of human life by which it is deprived of its eternal significance does not in the long run lead to unselfish service, but it leads to decadence and despair. At the very heart of the Christian religion, at any rate, despite what is being said today, is the hope of heaven. That hope is not selfish, but it is the highest and noblest thought, perhaps, that has ever been placed in the mind of man; it is the highest and noblest thought because it involves not mere selfish enjoyment but the glory of God. For the glory of God, realized through the creatures that He has made, eternity will not be too long. Man's chief end is not merely to glorify God and enjoy Him, but it is "to glorify God and to enjoy Him *for ever.*"

This thought of heaven runs all through the New Testament; and it is particularly prominent in the teaching of Jesus. Not only is it important in itself, moreover, but it has a very important bearing upon the

subject of the present little book. Faith is closely connected in the New Testament with hope; and it is contrasted in notable passages with sight. In contrast
with sight it is represented as a way by which we can
learn of things that are to be ours in the future world.
If, therefore, we are to understand in any adequate
manner what the New Testament says about faith, we
must attend very carefully to what the New Testament
says about heaven.

But we cannot understand at all what the New Testament says about heaven, unless we attend also to what
the New Testament says about hell; in the New Testament heaven and hell appear in contrast. That contrast
is found most clearly of all, strange though it may seem
to some persons, in the teaching of Jesus. Jesus speaks
not only about heaven but also, with very great plainness, about hell. "Fear not them which kill the body,"
said our Lord (to quote a typical utterance), "but are
not able to kill the soul: but rather fear him which is
able to destroy both soul and body in hell."[1]

These words were not spoken by Jonathan Edwards;
they were not spoken by Cotton Mather; they were not
spoken by Calvin, or by Augustine, or by Paul. But
they were spoken by Jesus.

And when they are put together with many other
words like them in the Gospels, they demonstrate the
utter falsity of the picture of Jesus which is being constructed in recent years. According to that picture,
Jesus preached what was essentially a religion of this
world; he advocated a filial attitude toward God and

[1] Matt. x: 28.

promoted a more abundant life of man, without being
interested in vulgar details as to what happens beyond
the grave; in the words of Professor Ellwood, he "concerned himself but little with the question of existence
after death."[2]

In order to destroy this picture, it is necessary only
to go through a Gospel harmony and note the passages
where Jesus speaks of blessedness and woe in a future
life. If you do that, you may be surprised at the result; certainly you will be surprised at the result if
you have previously been affected in slightest degree by
the misrepresentation of Jesus which dominates the
religious literature of our time. You will discover that
the thought not only of heaven but also the thought of
hell runs all through the teaching of Jesus.

It runs through the most characteristic parables of
Jesus— the solemn parables of the rich man and Laz-
arus, the unrighteous steward, the pounds, the talents,
the wheat and the tares, the evil servant, the marriage
of the king's son, the ten virgins. It is equally prominent in the rest of Jesus' teaching. The judgment
scene of the twenty-fifth chapter of Matthew is only
the culmination of what is found everywhere in the
Gospels: "These shall go away into everlasting punish-
ment: but the righteous into life eternal."[3] There is
absolutely nothing peculiar about this passage amid the
sayings of Jesus. If there ever was a religious teacher
who could not be appealed to in support of a religion

---

[2] Ellwood, *The Reconstruction of Religion*, 1922, p. 141.

[3] Matt. xxv: 46.

of this world, if there ever was a teacher who viewed the world under the aspect of eternity, it is Jesus of Nazareth.

These passages and a great mass of other passages like them are imbedded everywhere in the Gospel tradition. So far as I know even the most radical criticism has hardly tried to remove this element in Jesus' teaching. But it is not merely the amount of Jesus teaching about the future life which is impressive; what is even more impressive is the character of it. It does not appear as an excrescence in the Gospels, as something which might be removed and yet leave the rest of the teaching intact. If this element were removed, what would be left? Certainly not the gospel itself, certainly not the good news of Jesus' saving work; for that is concerned with these high issues of eternal life and death. But not even the ethical teaching of Jesus would be left. There can be no greater mistake than to suppose that Jesus ever separated theology from ethics, or that if you remove His theology—His beliefs about God and judgment, about future woe for the wicked and future blessedness for the good—you can have His ethical teaching intact. On the contrary, the stupendous earnestness of Jesus' ethics is rooted in the constant thought of the judgment seat of God. "And if thine eye offend thee, pluck it out, and cast it from thee: it is better for thee to enter into life with one eye, rather than having two eyes to be cast into hell fire."[4] These words are characteristic of all of Jesus' teaching; the stupendous earnestness of

[4] Matt. xviii: 9.

His commands is intimately connected with the alternative of eternal weal or woe.

That alternative is used by Jesus to arouse men to fear. "And fear not them which kill the body, but are not able to kill the soul: but rather fear him which is able to destroy both soul and body in hell."[5] Luke records a similar saying of Jesus: "And I say unto you my friends, Be not afraid of them that kill the body, and after that have no more than they can do. But I will forewarn you whom ye shall fear: Fear him, which after he hath killed hath power to cast into hell; yea, I say unto you, Fear him."[6] There are those who tell us that fear ought to be banished from religion; we ought, it is said, no longer to hold before men's eyes the fear of hell; fear, it is said, is an ignoble thing. Those who speak in this way certainly have no right to appeal to Jesus; for Jesus certainly did employ, and insistently, the motive of fear. If you eschew altogether that motive in religion, you are in striking contradiction to Jesus. Here, as at many other points, a choice must be made between the real Jesus and much that bears His name today. But who is right? Is Jesus right, or are those right who put out of their minds the fear of hell? Is fear altogether an ignoble thing; is a man necessarily degraded by being afraid?

I think that it depends altogether upon that of which one is afraid. The words of the text that we have been considering, with the solemn inculcation of fear,

[5] Matt. x: 28.
[6] Luke xii: 4 f.

are also a ringing denunciation of fear; the "Fear Him" is balanced by "Fear not." The fear of God is here made a way of overcoming the fear of man. And the heroic centuries of Christian history have provided abundant testimony to the efficaciousness of that way. With the fear of God before their eyes, the heroes of the faith have stood boldly before kings and governors and said: "Here I stand, I cannot do otherwise, God help me, Amen." It is certainly an ignoble thing to be afraid of bonds and death at the hands of men; it is certainly an ignoble thing to fear those who use power to suppress the right. Such fear has always been overcome by true men of faith.

Even the fear of God, indeed, might be degrading. It all depends upon what manner of being you hold God to be. If you think that God is altogether such an one as yourself, your fear of Him will be a degrading thing. If you think of Him as a capricious tyrant, envious of the creatures that He has made, you will never rise above the grovelling fears of Caliban. But it is very different when you stand in the presence of all the moral order in the universe; it is very different when God comes walking in the garden and you are without excuse; it is very different when you think of that dread day when your puny deceptions will fall off and you will stand defenceless before the righteous judgment throne. It is very different when not the sins of the other people but your own sins are being judged. Can we really come before the judgment seat of God and stand fearlessly upon our rights? Or can we really repeat with Henley the well-known words:

> Out of the night that covers me,
>   Black as the pit from pole to pole,
> I thank whatever gods may be
>   For my unconquerable soul.

or this:

> It matters not how strait the gate,
>   How charged with punishments the scroll,
> I am the master of my fate:
>   I am the captain of my soul.

Is this the way to overcome fear? Surely it is not. We can repeat such words only by the disguised cowardice of ignoring facts.

As a matter of fact, our soul is not unconquerable; we are not masters of our fate or captains of our soul. Many a man has contemplated some foul deed at first with horror, and said, "Am I a dog that I should do this thing?" And then has come the easy descent into the pit, the gradual weakening of the moral fibre, so that what seemed horrible yesterday seems excusable today; until at last, at some sad hour, with the memory of the horror of sin still in the mind, a man awakes to the realization that he is already wallowing in the mire. Such is the dreadful hardening that comes from sin. Even in this life we are not masters of our fate; we are of ourselves certainly not captains of our bodies, and we are of ourselves, I fear, not even captains of our souls.

It is pitiable cowardice to try to overcome fear by ignoring facts. We do not become masters of our fate by saying that we are. And such blatancy of pride.

futile as it is, is not even noble in its futility.   It
would be noble to rebel against a capricious tyrant; but
it is not noble to rebel against the moral law of God.

Are we, then, forever subject to fear?   Is there
naught, for us sinners, but a certain fearful looking
for of judgment and fiery indignation?   Jesus came to
tell us, No!   He came to deliver us from fear.   He did
not do so, indeed, by concealing facts; He painted no
false picture of the future life as a life of undifferen-
tiated futility such as that which the "mediums" reveal; He encouraged no false notion of a complacent
God who could make a compact with sin.   But he
delivered men from fear by leading them to trust in
Him.   Terrible is the issue of eternal life and eternal
death; woe to the man who approaches that issue in
his own righteousness; but Christ can enable us to
face even that.

Even the Christian, it is true, must fear God.   But
it is a new kind of fear.   It is a fear, at the most, of
chastisement and rebuke, not of final ruin; it is a fear,
indeed, rather of what might have been than of what
is; it is a fear of what would have come were we not
in Christ.   Without such fear there can be, for us sinners, no true love; for love of a saviour is proportioned
to one's horror of that from which one has been saved.
And how strong are the lives that are filled with such
a love!   They are lives brave not because the facts have
been ignored, but because they have been faced; they
are lives founded upon the solid foundation of the
grace of God.   If that is the foundation of our lives,
we shall not fear when we come to the hour that other-

wise we should dread. It is a beautiful thing when a Christian who has received Jesus as His Saviour comes to the moment of death; it is a beautiful thing to fall asleep in Jesus, and, as one enters that dark country of which none other can tell, to trust the dear Lord and Saviour and believe that we shall there see His face.

Thus faith is not merely founded upon knowledge; but also it leads to knowledge. It provides information about a future world that otherwise would be unknown. Our discussion would be incomplete if we did not examine a little more fully this aspect of faith.

The examination may be based upon one great verse in the Epistle to the Hebrews, in the chapter that deals expressly with faith. "Now faith," says the author of Hebrews at the beginning of that chapter, "is the substance of things hoped for, the evidence of things not seen."[7]

These words are not a definition or a complete account of faith: they tell what faith is, but they do not tell all that it is, and they do not separate it from all that it is not. There are other utterances also in the New Testament, which are sometimes treated as definitions and yet are not definitions at all. Thus when James says that "pure religion and undefiled before God and the Father is this, To visit the fatherless and widows in their affliction, and to keep himself unspotted from the world,"[8] he is not giving a definition or a complete description of religion; he is telling what religion is, but he is not telling all that it is: pure religion is to

7 Heb. xi: 1.
8 James i: 27.

visit the fatherless and widows and to keep himself
unspotted from the world, but it is far more than that.
Or when it is said that "God is love,"[9] that does not
mean at all that God is only love. It is a very great
logical error to single out such an affirmation and treat
it as though it were a definition; many such affirma-
tions would be necessary in order to obtain anything
like a complete account of God; God is love, but He is
many other things as well.

So when it is said that faith is "the substance of
things hoped for, the evidence of things not seen," that
does not mean that the substance of things hoped for
or the evidence of things not seen is always faith, or
that faith is only what it is here said to be. What we
have in this verse is not all of faith, but one particular
aspect of it. But since this particular aspect is an aspect which is usually being neglected today, this text
may perhaps be considered just now with special profit.
The aspect of faith which is here placed in the fore-
ground is one special part of the intellectual aspect of
it; faith is here regarded as contributing to the sum of
human knowledge.

At the present time it is the fashion to ignore this
aspect of faith: indeed faith and knowledge, as we have
already observed, are often divorced; they are treated
as though they belonged to two entirely different
spheres, and could therefore never by any chance come
either into relation or into contradiction. This separation between faith and knowledge has already been
considered so far as the basis of faith is concerned;

[9] I John iv: 8.

true faith, we have observed, is always based upon knowledge. But true faith is not only based upon knowledge, but also it leads to more knowledge; and it is this aspect of faith that is presented in classic form in the great verse at the beginning of the eleventh chapter of Hebrews.

"Faith," the author of Hebrews says, "is the substance of things hoped for." The word here translated "substance" is translated in the American Revised Version "assurance." But the difference is not important. The point in either case is that by faith future events are made to be certain; the old translation merely puts the thing a little more strongly: future events, it means, become through faith so certain that is as though they had already taken place; the things that are promised to us become, by our faith in the promise, so certain that it is as though we had the very substance of them in our hands here and now. In either case, whether the correct translation be "substance" or "assurance," faith is here regarded as providing information about future events; it is presented as a way of predicting the future.

There are various ways of predicting the future; faith is one way, but it is not the only way. Another way is provided, for example, by astronomy. On the twenty-fourth day of January, 1925, there was visible in the eastern part of the United States a total eclipse of the sun. Elaborate preparations were made in order to take observations; the experts were so firmly convinced that the eclipse would take place that large sums of money were invested on the basis of the conviction. In connection with another eclipse that took place a few years before, even more expensive preparations were made. On that occasion the eclipse was visible in a much less accessible region, and various expeditions had to be sent many thousands of miles in order that the observations might be made; the astronomers seemed very firmly convinced indeed that the eclipse would take place.

It is true that in some cases the labor was all wasted. In the places to which some of the expeditions went it rained or was cloudy; bad weather spoiled those elaborate scientific expeditions just as effectually as if they had been any ordinary Sunday School picnics. It may be, of course, that scientific men will learn to eliminate even this source of error; it may be that they will learn to predict with certainty, or even control, the weather. We certainly hope that it will not come in our day. For if it comes in our day, no doubt the farmers' bloc will want one kind of weather and the industrial workers another, so that what is now almost the only really safe topic of casual conversation will become a cause of civil war. But although the weather could not be predicted long enough ahead, and although it obscured the eclipse, yet no doubt the eclipse did take place on schedule time. On the last occasion, I believe, the eclipse was four seconds late: but those four seconds did not trouble me nearly so much as they troubled the astronomers; from my layman's point of view I am bound to say that I think the astronomers had succeeded fairly well in their way of predicting the future.

But although astronomy is one way of predicting the future, and a very good way too, it is not the only way. Another way is faith. And what ought to be observed with special care is that faith is just as scientific as astronomy. The future is predicted by means of faith when one depends for one's knowledge of the future on the word of a personal being. And in ordinary life that method of prediction is constantly employed. Upon it depends, for example, the entire orderly conduct of economic, political and social life. Business is carried on by means of credit, and it is perfectly scientific to carry it on so; it is perfectly scientific to hold that reputable men of business, especially when they eliminate personal idiosyncrasies by acting collectively, will meet their obligations. Political life is possible only by faith reposed in the government, and where such faith is destroyed one has hopeless anarchy. Social life is possible only because of faith— social life in its larger aspects and also in the humblest and most individual details. It is really just as scientific to predict that a mother will give the medicine at the proper time to her sick baby as it is to predict an eclipse of the sun. No doubt there are more disturbing factors in the former case than in the latter, and no doubt those disturbing factors must be duly taken into account; but that does not affect the essentially sound scientific character of the prediction. In any ideally complete scientific mapping out of the future course of the world the probability that the mother would give the medicine to the baby would have to be taken into account just as truly as the probability of the eclipse of the sun.

Sometimes a prediction as to the future conduct of a person can be established with a certain degree of mathematical precision: it is discovered that a certain person has met his obligations in ninety-nine out of a hundred past cases; the probabilities, therefore, it will be said, are strongly in favor of his meeting his obligations in a similar case in the future. Certain forms of liability insurance, I imagine (though I know very little about it), are based upon some such calculation. But very often one's predictions as to the future conduct of a person, though attaining a very high degree of probability indeed, are not based upon any such merely mathematical reasoning: a person sometimes inspires confidence by his entire bearing; soul speaks to soul; and even apart from long experience of that person's trustworthiness one knows that he is to be trusted. That kind of trust has a larger place, by the way, in producing Christian conviction than is sometimes supposed. Even that kind of trust is thoroughly reasonable; it adds to the sum-total of knowledge, and is in a true sense of the word "scientific." Common experience bears out the words of the text that faith is "the substance of things hoped for."

The text also says that faith is the "evidence of things not seen." That assertion includes the other. Future things—the things hoped for—are always also "things not seen." The Christian, for example, in thinking of his communion in heaven with Christ, walks by faith not by sight; because he does not now see heaven. He has not the evidence of his eyes, but needs confidence in Christ to make heaven real to him.

But this second affirmation of the text, though it includes the first, goes also beyond it; faith is sometimes needed not only to predict the future but also to give information about hidden things that already exist. Whether the information concerns the future or the present, it is based upon faith if it depends upon the word of a personal being.

Faith, then, though it has other aspects, is always, if it be true faith, a way of obtaining knowledge; it should never be contrasted with science. Indeed, in any true universal science—a science that would obliterate the artificial departmental boundaries which we have erected for purposes of convenience and as a concession to human limitations—in any true universal science, confidence in personal beings would have a recognized place as a means of obtaining knowledge just as truly as chemical balances or telescopes.

It is therefore only with great caution that we can accept the distinction set up by Tennyson at the beginning of *In Memoriam*:

> Strong Son of God, immortal Love,
> Whom we, that have not seen thy face,
> By faith, and faith alone, embrace,
> Believing where we cannot prove.

"Believing where we cannot prove"—it all depends upon what you mean by "prove." If you mean by "prove" "obtain knowledge by your own observation without depending upon information received from other persons," then of course the distinction between belief (or faith) and proof is valid, and it may readily be admitted that in that sense the Christian religion depends upon faith rather than upon proof. But what ought to be insisted upon above all things is that "belief" or faith, in the Tennysonian sense, may afford just as high a degree of scientific certitude as "proof" —in the narrower sense of the word. Indeed in countless cases it affords a much higher degree of certitude. Perhaps the reader may pardon an illustration from ordinary life. I have an account at one of the Princeton banks. It is not so large an account as I should like, but it is there. Every month the bank sends me a report as to my balance. I also obtain information as to the same thing by the calculation which I make on the stubs of my check book. The information which I obtain by my own calculation is obtained by "proof" in the Tennysonian sense (or the sense which rightly or wrongly we have attributed to Tennyson). The information which I obtain from the bank, on the other hand, is obtained by faith—it depends upon my confidence in the accuracy and integrity of the employees of the bank. I have not the slightest notion how the banks attain such a marvellous degree of accuracy. One of the first teachers of mathematics that I ever had told me, I think, something to the effect that the officials of a bank sometimes spend the entire night searching the books for one cent that is unaccounted for. Recently I think I read in the *Saturday Evening Post* or some such journal, to my great disappointment, that if they are only one cent off they go to bed. It was a youthful idol shattered! At any rate I do not know how they do it; I have not at all followed the steps of their calculation of my balance: yet I take the result

with perfect confidence. It is a pure matter of faith.
Now not infrequently at the end of a month differences
of opinion emerge, I am sorry to say, between the bank
and myself as to the amount of my balance; "faith"
in the bank's report is pitted against "proof" as based
on my own calculations. And the curious thing is
that faith is much stronger, much more scientific, than
proof. I used to think that my calculation might be
right and the bank's report wrong, but now I trust the
bank every time. It is true, I have the desire to make
the two means of obtaining knowledge converge; I
have the intellectual desire of financially unifying my
world. But I do so not by correcting the bank's report
but by correcting my own calculation. I correct "proof"
because I have obtained better information by "faith."

That case, simple as it is, illustrates, I think, a great
principle which goes to the vitals of religion. It is not
true that convictions based on the word of others must
necessarily be less firm and less scientific than convictions
based on one's own calculation and observation. One's
own calculation and observation may turn out to be
wrong as well as one's confidence in the word of another
person

So it is in the case of the Christian religion. The
central convictions of the Christian religion, at least
so far as the gospel of salvation is concerned, are based
not upon our own observation, but upon testimony;
they are based, in the first place, upon the testimony of
the Biblical writers as to things said and done in the
first century of our era in Palestine. That testimony
may conceivably be true and it may conceivably be

false; but to say beforehand that it cannot be true is to fall into a very serious intellectual fault. If the testimony is true, then the rejection of it is just as unscientific and the acceptance of it just as scientific as the rejection or acceptance of assured results in the field of the laboratory sciences.

As a matter of fact, we Christians think that the testimony is true. Why do we think so? No doubt there are various reasons; we test the assertions of the Biblical writers in many different ways before we accept them finally as true. But one reason has sometimes not been given quite the degree of prominence that it deserves. One very important reason for accepting the testimony of the New Testament about Christ is that we become personally acquainted with the writers who give us the testimony and on the basis of that acquaintance come to have an overpowering impression that they are telling us the truth. If you are troubled with doubts about the truth of the New Testament, if these marvellous things seem to you too strange ever really to have happened upon this earth, I should like to commend to you an exercise that has been helpful to me; I should like to suggest to you the plan of reading rapidly great sections of the Gospel narrative as though for the first time. The Gospel of Mark, for example, lends itself readily to this purpose; perhaps that is the reason why God has given us one Gospel that is so short. Read the Gospel of Mark all through, then, in one sitting; do not *study* it this time (important though detailed study at other times will be found to be), but simply *read* it; simply let the total impression of it be

made upon your mind. If you do that you will feel
that you have become well acquainted with the author;
and you will have an overpowering impression that he
is telling the truth. It is inconceivable, you will say,
that this stupendous picture of Jesus could ever have
been the product of invention or of the myth-making
fancy of the Church; the author of the Gospel of Mark,
if he could be placed upon the witness-stand, would
make an overpoweringly good witness, and would bring
conviction to the mind of any jury that was open to
the facts.

The same thing may be done also in the case of a book
that is so much attacked as is the Fourth Gospel. In
the course of my life, if a personal allusion may be par-
doned, I have read a great deal that has been written
against the historical trustworthiness of that book.
Some of it at times has seemed to me to be plausible;
I have been troubled at times by serious doubts. But
at such times I have turned away from what has been
written about the book to the book itself; I have tried
to read it as though for the first time. And when I
have done that, the impression has sometimes been quite
overpowering. Clearly the author is claiming to be an
eyewitness, and clearly he lays special stress upon the
plain testimony of the senses. If he was not really an
eyewitness of the life of Jesus, he is engaging in a refined piece of deception, vastly more heinous than if
he had merely put a false name at the beginning of his
book. That he is engaging in such a piece of deception
may seem plausible when one merely reads what has
been written about the author by others; but it seems

to be a truly monstrous hypothesis when one gets personally acquainted with the author by reading his book
for one's self.   When one does that, the conviction
becomes overpowering that this author was actually, as
he claims to be, an eyewitness of the wondrous things
that he narrates, that he actually beheld the glory
of the incarnate Word, and that the stupendous Person
of whom he writes actually walked upon this earth.

To neglect this kind of evidence—the kind of evidence that is based upon personal testimony—is, we
maintain, a thoroughly unscientific thing.   There is a
breadth and open-mindedness about true science of
which many persons seem not to have the slightest conception.   They become immersed in one kind of evidence; within one limited sphere, their observations are
good: but with regard to other kinds of evidence they
are totally blind.   Such blindness needs to be overcome
if we are to have real scientific advance; the true scientist has his mind open not merely to some, but to all,
of the facts.   And if he has his eye open to all of the
facts, he will not neglect what is told him by credible
witnesses with regard to Jesus Christ.

Still less can we neglect, if we be truly scientific men,
what is told us by Jesus Himself.   The New Testament writers tell us about Jesus; on the basis of their
testimony we are convinced that the Jesus of the New
Testament really lived in this world, that He really
died for our sins, that He really rose from the dead,
and is now living so that He can be our Saviour.   If
we have accepted that testimony about Jesus, then we
have Jesus Himself; and if we have Jesus Himself, it is

reasonable to trust Him not only for this world but also for the world to come.

It is highly misleading, therefore, to say that religion and science are separate, and that the Bible is not intended to teach science. No doubt that assertion that the Bible is not intended to teach science does contain an element of truth: it is certainly true that there are many departments of science into which the Bible does not enter; and very possibly it is advantageous to isolate certain departments provisionally and pursue investigations in those departments without for the moment thinking of others. But such isolation is at the best provisional merely; and ultimately there ought to be a real synthesis of truth. On principle, it cannot be denied that the Bible does teach certain things about which science has a right to speak. The matter is particularly clear in the sphere of history. At the very centre of the Bible are assertions about events in the external world in Palestine in the first century of our era—events the narrating of which constitutes the "gospel," the piece of good news upon which our Christian faith is based. But events in Palestine in the first century of our era are just as much a proper subject for scientific history as are events in Greece or Rome. And in an ideally complete scientific account of the physical universe the emergence or non-emergence of the body of Jesus from the tomb—a question upon which the very existence of Christianity depends—would have to be recorded just as truly as the observations that are made in the laboratory.

We shall have to reject, therefore, the easy apologetic

for Christianity which simply declares that religion and science belong in independent spheres and that science can never conceivably contradict religion. Of course real science can never actually contradict any religion that is true; but to say, before the question is determined whether the religion is true or false, that science cannot possibly contradict it, is to do despite both to religion and to science. It is a poor religion that can abandon to science the whole realm of objective truth, in order to reserve for itself merely a realm of ideals. Such a religion, at any rate, whatever estimate may be given of it, is certainly not Christianity; for Christianity is founded squarely, not merely upon ideals, but upon facts. But if Christianity is founded upon facts, then it is not entirely independent of science; for all facts must be brought into some sort of relation. When any new fact enters the human mind it must proceed to make itself at home; it must proceed to introduce itself to the previous denizens of the house. That process of introduction of new facts is called thinking. And, contrary to what seems to be quite generally supposed, thinking cannot be avoided by the Christian man. The Christian religion is not an innocent but useless epiphenomenon, without interrelation with other spheres of knowledge, but must seek to justify its place, despite all the intellectual labor that that costs, in the realm of facts.

Let us, however, have no fear. Our religion is really founded upon words of soberness and truth; it suffers just now not from an excess of thinking, but from a woeful deficiency of it, and a true broadening of knowledge would lead again into faith. It is, of course, a mistake to apply to one science the methods of another; perhaps that is the reason why men who are experts in the sphere of the laboratory sciences are often so very unscientific when they come to deal, for example, with history. Moreover the evidence for the truth of Christianity is very varied, and it is not all of a kind that can easily be reduced to measurement. The Gospel witness to Jesus, for example, is wonderfully convincing when one attends to it in the way that such evidence requires; it is wonderfully convincing when one brings it into connection with the facts of the soul. The evidence in favor of that Gospel witness, moreover, is cumulative; it will not lightly be rejected by anyone who really has an open mind. And when, by accepting that witness about Jesus, we have Jesus Himself, still more clearly can we trust Him for time and for eternity. The witness is confirmed here and now by present expecrience; the Christian knows the One in whom He has believed. Faith need not be too humble or too apologetic before the bar of reason; Christian faith is a thoroughly reasonable thing; it is, as the Epistle to the Hebrews puts it, "the substance of things hoped for, the evidence of things not seen."

Our treatment of faith is nearly at an end. But one very practical question remains. Faith, we have seen, is the appointed means of salvation; without it there is—at least for those who have come to years of discretion—no saving contact with Christ. But faith is sometimes strong and sometimes weak: how strong, then, does it have to be in order that a soul may be saved?

In answer to this question, it must certainly be admitted that the New Testament does recognize varying degrees of faith; and it does seek with great earnestness to make faith strong instead of weak. According to the New Testament a strong, firm faith unmixed by doubts is something that is used by God to accomplish great things. The matter is particularly plain in the case of prayer; the efficacy of prayer, according to the New Testament, does depend to some extent upon the degree of faith that is given to the man who prays; a weak, trembling faith is not ordinarily the instrument that removes mountains and casts them into the sea. But there is another aspect of the New Testament teaching; and it should not be neglected if we are to have comfort in the Christian life. Though God can use a firm, strong faith exercised in prayer, he also often uses a faith that is very weak. It is a great mistake to think that prayer works in any mechanical way; so that while a good prayer brings a good result a poor prayer necessarily brings a poor result. On the contrary, the efficacy of prayer depends after all not upon the excellence of the prayer but upon the grace of God, and often God is pleased to honor prayers that are very faulty indeed. Thank God that it is so; thank God that though we know not what we should pray for as we ought His Spirit "maketh intercession for us with groanings which cannot be uttered"; thank God that He does for us not in proportion as we ask, but "exceeding abundantly above all that we ask or think."

Thus it is, then, with prayer: there must be some faith if prayer is to be prayer at all and not a meaningless form of words; but even weak faith is sometimes, in God's infinite mercy, used to accomplish great things. But if it is thus with the details of the Christian life, if it is thus with prayer, how is it with salvation? Faith is necessary to salvation, but how much faith is necessary? How does God treat the man of little faith?

In answer to this question we have in the Gospels a wonderful incident with which the present little attempt at exposition of the New Testament teaching about faith may fitly close.

The incident is the healing of the demoniac boy in the ninth chapter of the Gospel according to Mark.[10] It is also contained in Matthew and Luke as well as in Mark, but in very much briefer form. It is Mark alone who paints the picture in detail; it is Mark far more than the other two who enables us to see with the eyes of those who were present at the scene. If early Christian tradition be right, as no doubt it is right, in holding that the Second Gospel embodies the missionary preaching of Peter, then the vivid character of the narrative is explained. The evangelist enables us to see with Peter's eyes. Peter with two other disciples had been upon the Mount of Transfiguration; he had seen the Lord in glory with Moses and Elias; and now on the descent from the mountain he tells us, through the words of the second Gospel, exactly what he saw below. Mark has preserved the details; he has made no attempt at stylistic smoothness; his narrative is rough and vigorous and natural. Nowhere is Mark more characteristically Marcan than here.

10 Mark ix: 14-29.

As thus depicted the scene is a scene of human misery
and need. A man was in distress; his son was in the
grip of an evil spirit, he foamed at the mouth and
gnashed his teeth and now lay wallowing on the
ground. In the presence of this distress, men were
powerless to help; even the disciples of Jesus, despite all
the power of their Master, could do nothing. It is a
picture of human need and the powerlessness of man.
And the scene has not been made antiquated today.
The cause of the ill then, I believe, was different from
that which is observed at the present time; but the re-
sulting misery was in important respects the same. Med-
ical science has not yet gotten rid of human misery; and
it is quite inconceivable that it ever will succeed in doing
so. No doubt the form of misery may be changed; it
is perfectly conceivable, though perhaps highly improb-
able, that disease may be conquered. But death, at
least, in the present order, will remain; and with death
and bereavement there will be the distressed cry of the
human soul.

The man in the Marcan scene was at the very extrem-
ity of distress. All resources had failed, and misery
was at its height. And then Jesus came down from
the mountain. In Him was a new and the very last
resource. But Jesus did not help at once. The means
of his helping was faith, and did the man believe? "If
thou canst do anything," said the man; and it was a
despairing rather than a believing "if." But Jesus did
not despair. Faith was not apparent, but Jesus knew
how to bring it forth; he brought to light the faith
which the man possessed. "How long is it ago," he

said, "since this came into him?" And then he said, to call faith forth: "All things are possible to him that believeth."

The answer of the man is one of the unforgettable utterances of the human spirit; it will remain classic so long as the race endures. It is not merely the voice of one man, but it voices the cry of the race. Thus, I suppose, out of wild distress, do many great utterances come. Ordinary speech covers the thought in conventional trappings; but in times of overpowering emotion the form of expression is forgotten and a cry comes unbidden and unshaped from the depths of the soul.

So it was with the man of this incident. Concealment was forgotten; there was no pretence of a confidence which was not possessed; there was no attempt at logical harmony between the faith and the unbelief that struggled unreconciled in the soul. "Lord I believe," said the man; "help thou mine unbelief." That was the faith, weak faith it is true, that was born of need.

So must all faith, I suppose, be born. I do not mean that faith in Christ cannot come without previous anguish of soul. Some children of Christian homes believe in their Saviour almost as soon as full consciousness begins; and that simple faith of childhood remains sometimes grandly unshaken through all the storms of life. But hosts of men today do not believe in Christ at all. How shall they be led to faith in Him? We have already seen what the answer is;[11] they can be led only through the sense of need.

11 See Chapter IV.

The need of the man in the Gospel of Mark was plain. His son was gnashing with the teeth and wallowing on the ground. But the need of all men, if they could only discern the facts, is equally clear. The great need of the human soul which leads to faith in Christ is found, as we have seen, in the fact of sin. A man never accepts Christ as Saviour unless he knows himself to be in the grip of the demon of sin and desires to be set free. One may argue with a man on the subject of religion as long as life endures; one may bring forward arguments for the existence of a personal God; one may attempt to prove on the basis of the documentary evidence that only the Christian view of Christ and only His resurrection from the tomb can explain the origin of the Christian religion. Men will listen, if they be broad-minded (as, however, they seldom are today); but repelled by the stupendous nature of the thing that we ask them to believe, they will reject all our arguments and conviction will not be formed. But then, as we despair of bringing them ever to faith, we receive sometimes an unexpected ally. In some unexpected way the hollowness and hopelessness of their lives comes home to them; they recognize the awful guilt of sin. And when that recognition comes, the proofs of the Christian religion suddenly obtain for them a new cogency; everything in the Christian system falls for them into its proper place; and they believe. Belief in Christ, today as always, can be attained only when there is a sense of need.

That does not mean that we despise the external proofs of the Christian religion. They are absolutely

necessary; without them the sense of need would lead
only to despair. It is one of the root errors of the present day to suppose that because the philosophical and
historical foundations of our religion are insufficient to
produce faith, they are therefore unnecessary. The truth
is that their insufficiency is due not at all to any weakness of their own but only to a weakness in our minds.
Pragmatism should be avoided by the Christian with all
the energy of his soul, as indeed it should be avoided
by everyone who will not acquiesce in the present lamentable intellectual decline which pragmatism has
brought about. The facts of the Christian religion remain facts no matter whether we cherish them or not:
they are facts for God; they are facts both for angels
and for demons; they are facts now, and they will
remain facts beyond the end of time.

But, as we have observed in an earlier part of our
discussion, the facts are one thing, and the recognition
of the facts is another. And it is the recognition of the
facts that depends for us upon the sense of need. The
man who has come to discern the sin of his own soul,
who has stripped aside the miserable conventional ex-
cuses for sin and seen himself as God sees him, is a man
who like a drowning person will snatch at a plank that
may save him from the abyss. Without the sense of
dire need the stupendous, miraculous events of Jesus'
coming and Jesus' resurrection are unbelievable because
they are out of the usual order; but to the man who
knows the terrible need caused by sin these things are
valuable just because they are out of the usual order.
The man who is under the conviction of sin can accept

the supernatural; for He knows that there is an adequate occasion for its entrance into the course of this world.

Bring even modern men to a real sense of sin, and despite all the prejudice against the gospel story, they will be led to cry at least: "Lord, I believe; help thou mine unbelief." That cry of the distressed man in Mark was not the cry of perfect faith. But through it the man was saved. So it will be today. Even very imperfect and very weak faith is sufficient for salvation; salvation does not depend upon the strength of our faith, but it depends upon Christ. When you want assurance of salvation, think not about your faith, but about the Person who is the object of your faith. Faith is not a force that does something, but it is a channel by which something is received. Once let that channel be opened, and salvation comes in never to depart. It is a great mistake to suppose that Christians win through to salvation because they maintain themselves by their own efforts in an attitude of faith. On the contrary, saving faith means putting one's trust once for all in Christ. He will never desert those who are committed to Him, but will keep them safe both in this world and in that which is to come.

In the second part of Bunyan's *Pilgrim's Progress* there is one of those unforgettable portraits which have caused the book of the tinker of Bedford—that tenderest and most theological of English books—to be one of the true masterpieces of the world's literature. It is the portrait of "Mr. Fearing." Mr. Fearing had "the root of the matter" in him; he was a true Christian. But he got little comfort out of his religion. When he came to the Interpreter's house, he was afraid to go in; he lay trembling outside till he was almost starved. But then, when at last he was brought in, he received a warm welcome. "I will say that for my Lord," said Great-heart, "he carried it wonderful lovingly to him." And so Mr. Fearing went moaningly on his way; and when he was come to the entrance of the Valley of the Shadow of Death, "I thought," said the guide, "I should have lost my man." At last he came to the River which all must cross, and there he was in a heavy case. "Now, now, he said, he should be drowned for ever, and so never see that face with comfort that he had come so many miles to behold." But never, we are told, had the water of that River been seen so low as it was on the day that Mr. Fearing went across. "So he went over at last, not much above wet-shod. When he was going up to the Gate, Mr. Great-heart began to take his leave of him, and to wish him a good reception above. So he said, *I shall, I shall.*"

Such is the blessed end of the man even of little faith. Weak faith will not remove mountains, but there is one thing at least that it will do; it will bring a sinner into peace with God. Our salvation does not depend upon the strength of our faith; saving faith is a channel not a force. If you are once really committed to Christ, then despite your subsequent doubts and fears you are His for ever.

THE END.

INDEX

INDEX

I. NAMES AND SUBJECTS

INDEX

58; Christianity is a way of getting rid of, 110; the consciousness of, necessary to faith, 118-142, 248-250; the fact of, must not be ignored in the intellectual approach to Christ, 132-136; the consciousness of, is necessary to the esthetic approach to Christ, 136f., is necessary to the approach to Christ through the desire for companionship, 137-139, is necessary to the approach to Christ through the desire for an ideal, 34f., is necessary to the understanding of the atonement, 144; salvation from the power of, 204; the teaching of Paul about presence of, in Christians, 207; the existence of, is denied in the modern world, 214-216.
Social life, is possible only because of faith, 233.
Socialism, 212.
Son of Man, the, 109.
Spencer, Herbert, 35f.
Stoicism, 122.
Students, theological, 22, 42.
Sunday Schools, 23.
Supernatural, the; see under "Miracles."

Tennyson, 71, 235f.
Terminology, theoogical, 161-163.
Testimony, is at the basis of the Christian religion, 237-240.
Theism, 47-66, 84, 131.
Theology: falsely distinguished from religion, 28-39; is a

science, 33; is regarded by Modernists as the symbolic expression of experience, 28-39; abandonment of, involves abandonment of Christianity, 39f.; intrusion of, into Christianity, according to Dr. McGiffert, 57.
Theory of the atonement, the, realtion of, to the fact, 144-148.
Thinking, facts are necessary to, 19f.
Toplady, 194.
Transcendence of God, 53, 65.
Translations, modern, of the New Testament, 162.
Trinity, the, all three Persons of, are objects of faith, 87.
Truth: objectivity of, 32ff.; relation of, to faith, 174-180.

Undergraduates, modern, 16f.

Virgin birth, the, 91.
Volitional aspect of faith, the, 135f.

Waterhouse, E. S., 35f.
Weather, possible control of the, 232
Wells, H. G., 54.
Westminster Confession, 30, 34.
Westminster Standards, 36.
Westminster Shorter Catechism, 36, 135f., 147, 151f., 221.
Wonder, is not destroyed by the knowledge of God, 65f.
Works, the relation of, to faith, 183-218.
Woman's Home Companion, The, 6.

II. BIBLICAL PASSAGES

OLD TESTAMENT

NEW TESTAMENT